THE SAMURAI
AND THE
POWER OF 7

THE SAMURAI AND THE POWER OF 7

Copyright © 2022 by Robert G. Chu

Front and Back Cover Design by TK Palad

All Right Reserved.

No part of this publication may be reproduced, distributed, or transmitted in any form or by any means, including photocopying, recording, or other electronic or mechanical methods, or by any information storage and retrieval system without the prior written permission of the publisher, except in the case of very brief quotations embodied in critical reviews and certain other non-commercial uses permitted by copyright law.

Printed in the United States of America

THE SAMURAI AND THE POWER OF 7

BECOME THE HIGHEST VERSION OF YOURSELF

LIVE YOUR SUPREME DESTINY

ROBERT G. CHU

To my wife and best friend, Dianne, your light and your energy are medicine to me.

To my sons and daughter, I humbly dedicate this book to you. What matters most in life is love, everything else is trivial.

"All journeys outward ultimately lead to the journey inward, where everything you seek already exists and awaits your joyous acceptance."

"Behind every choice, the only real choice is between fear and love. Fear hurts and Love heals. Boil every choice down to what heals versus what hurts, answer fear with love and you will find the peace you seek."

–A Course in Miracles made easy, Alan Cohen

"There is a supreme moment of destiny calling on your life. Your job is to feel that, to hear that, to know that."

-Oprah Winfrey

CONTENTS

PROLOGUE	1
CHAPTER 1: The Unfulfilled Samurai	3
CHAPTER 2: The Perfect Katana	15
CHAPTER 3: The Master of Letting Go	25
CHAPTER 4: The Architect and the Cherry Blossom	49
CHAPTER 5: The Fisherman with No Regrets	65
CHAPTER 6: The Worthy Warrior	83
CHAPTER 7: The Purposeful Priest	95
CHAPTER 8: The Shogun and the Power of his Mind	107
CHAPTER 9: The Final Master	125
CHAPTER 10: The Samurai and the Power of 7	139
EPILOGUE	143
ABOUT THE AUTHOR	145

PROLOGUE

The only sound you could hear is the breath of the Samurai who had fallen to his knees in the open field surrounded by white and pink cherry blossoms that had slowly fallen from the Sakura trees above. He had trouble opening his left eye, not knowing if the pain was from the rain or blood dripping into it from the new wound on the top of his head. His left hand was putting pressure on his abdomen, knowing he may be breathing his last breaths, and yet he remained calm and even more determined. His right hand clutched his katana, a sacred sword with the words "Power of 7" surrounded by 7 circles engraved on the base of the blue-tinged blade, given to him by his father before he died.

At 42 years old, Hitoshi Tabata had accomplished so much in his life. He had a youthful appearance, and if it weren't for the sadness in his eyes and the calluses on his hands, one would never know how much he had to endure to get to this moment. A year ago, Hitoshi defeated his 200th opponent, cementing his legacy as one of the most feared and respected Samurai in Japan. Despite having this title and accomplishing what many could only dream of, Hitoshi felt an emptiness inside he couldn't explain that no victory or accomplishment could ever fill.

He had been in hundreds of battles before, but this was different. The hooded Samurai standing across from him had killed his sister many years ago. This battle was personal for Hitoshi, who knew he was running out of time. He had to use the principles of the Power of 7 he learned from the seven Master Samurai to unleash one last strike using the little energy he had left.

A few yards away stood a much older Samurai. He wore a large black hood that covered half his face. Underneath the hood, you could see a glimpse of the older Samurai's cold eyes and blank stare. His skin was weathered, almost leathery. The deep lines on his face portrayed a man who had led a difficult and painful life. There was a coldness to his aura. Unlike Hitoshi, this battle was not personal to the hooded Samurai. Hitoshi Tabata would be just another Samurai he's killed, besides countless women and children he's killed before. The hooded Samurai stood upright with his right hand gripping tightly on the handle of his cold blade that appeared hungry for flesh, with a drop of fresh blood dripping from its sharp metal tip. The hooded Samurai knew it wouldn't be long before he defeated the great Hitoshi Tabata.

CHAPTER 1

The Unfulfilled Samurai

Hitoshi Tabata grew up in a small traditional village called Shakujii. The exterior of the village was filled with inns, teahouses and shops that sold everything from waxes, soy sauce and silk. As the sun rose, the smell of fish, vegetables and chestnuts would fill the air as the village came to life. The village's craftsmen were known for their unique technique of producing urushi, also known as lacquerware. This knowledge came from generations of experience and a complex procedure of extracting the sap of the lacquer tree, which in its purest form is highly poisonous and gently heating it to remove all toxicity and excess moisture. Once hardened, the lacquer has a unique luster that can be applied to wood, glass, fabric and even paper to create beautiful and durable items such as tableware, artwork and even furniture.

Travelers from all over Japan would travel to Shakujii village in search of the highest quality handmade lacquerware. The village, however, was most known for a beautiful small open field in the center surrounded by large weeping cherry blossom trees known as Sakura Trees in Japan. Every year in the Spring, the cherry blossoms would bloom for 1 to 2 weeks, and there would be an explosion of white and pink flowers surrounding the field. Visitors to Shakujii would enter the field and be temporarily transported to a serene, calm and tranquil world where they could reflect and appreciate the beauty surrounding them.

A path leading to a clear turquoise lake was at the village's end. The path was lined with 5-foot high stone lanterns on both sides. Azalea shrubs of different sizes lined the ground next to the stone lanterns and mature Japanese Maple trees that were hundreds of years old stood tall behind them. In the fall, you could see a canopy of green, red and yellow leaves from the trees above and a burst of purple, pink and white from the azalea shrubs on the ground as you walked down the path.

Hitoshi's parents and sister called him Toshi for short. They lived in a small home with tatami flooring made from grass woven around a rice straw core that kept the flooring firm. When Toshi was born, he had a hemangioma growing on the left side of his head that appeared to be a small blister filled with blood. His mother, who was already a slightly neurotic and anxious person, to begin with, worried daily about the blister popping and grew to be overly protective of her little boy.

His father dreamed of becoming a respected warrior in his youth but quickly gave up his dreams because he didn't have the physical attributes to become one. He made up for what he lacked in physical abilities in mental and strategic capability. His father was a student of martial arts and knew how to dislocate every bone in someone's body in at least 3 ways using technique and leverage. He also knew every successful combat and battle strategy. His father had high hopes for both his children and aimed to impart all his knowledge to them.

Toshi shared a bedroom with his older sister, whom he adored and idolized. She was fearless and stronger than most children her age. She would never back down from a fight and always protect Toshi from neighboring children when they made fun of the red birthmark on the side of his head. Toshi loved sitting on the tatami floor watching his older sister train with their father and couldn't wait for the day he could join them.

When Toshi turned 7 years old, the hemangioma on his head had receded leaving only a small circular area that was more tender than the surrounding skin. He would never forget his father saying, "It's time for Toshi to begin his training in Jiu-Jitsu and the Art of the Sword."

"He's too young and fragile to learn," he remembers his mother saying. "He is too weak to beat anyone in battle. He will never be strong enough to be a great warrior."

"He is stronger than you know, and if he is going to be a respected Samurai when he grows up, he needs to begin training now," Toshi's father replied. "No more waiting, no more excuses, his training begins today!"

Toshi loved to train. He desperately wanted to make his parents and his sister proud. He wanted to prove to them he wasn't too fragile and that he wasn't too weak. He cleaned the tatami flooring early every morning and patiently waited for his father and sister to arrive. He loved having his sister as his training partner. Toshi trained hard and never wanted to give up by tapping out, an act of tapping the mat or his training partner twice to let them know you were giving up and "submitting" to them. Even when his sister would have him in a joint lock, Toshi refused to tap out no matter how much pain he was in. He was determined to prove to his parents he was strong and a capable warrior. No matter how strong Toshi thought he was, his sister was always a step ahead and would easily get him in a submission hold when they trained. Toshi appreciated that his sister would always let go of the hold when their father was watching, making it seem like Toshi had successfully defended himself and escaped on his own.

In the evenings, Toshi anxiously waited in bed for his father to tell them the story of the Samurai Masters and the Power of 7. His father would light a candle next to their bed, wrap them both in warm blankets and tell the story in the exact same way each time. "Once upon a time, there were 7 Samurai Masters. Each Master had the secret to removing blockages to a specific energy center in your body. Once you were able to release all 7 blockages, you would have the ability to become the highest version of yourself and reach your highest potential both in battle and in life."

Toshi slept every night, dreaming about Samurai Masters and energy centers. He idolized the stories of famous Samurai in history, such as Tokugawa Ieyasu. Tokugawa Ieyasu was one of the most powerful daimyo in his time. Daimyo were feudal warlords who controlled large provinces and had Samurai to protect their land and property. Tokugawa Ieyasu's rise to power was legendary, and he became the founder and first Shogun of the Tokugawa Shogunate. Although Shogun were hereditary military leaders appointed by the emperor, they were the ones with real power who made governmental decisions and worked closely with Japanese society. Tokugawa Ieyasu was considered one of the Great Unifiers of Japan.

When Toshi turned 16 years old, it was already obvious that he was a gifted fighter. He not only had the mental and strategic knowledge of his father, but he also had the physical attributes to become a great warrior. He was easily recognizable by everyone in the village since he was already taller and stronger than men twice his age. He wore his hair in a chonmage, a traditional hairstyle by Samurai warriors, with his hair tied up in a top knot on top of his head. He would often walk around the village wearing a Jingasa, a triangle-shaped bamboo hat to stay cool in the heat.

He had become an expert in Jiu-Jitsu and utilized all the techniques he learned from his father. Toshi knew all the ways to choke and submit an opponent, using a stronger part of his own body to control, manipulate and dislocate the smaller joints of his opponents. Though most considered Toshi's Jiu-Jitsu one of the best in the village, he was even a better swordsman with the ability and intuition to predict his opponent's strikes and counter them easily.

The traditional and most common way to hold a Katana, a Japanese sword characterized by a curved single-edged blade, was to hold it with the blade facing up since it allowed the holder to maintain their distance from their opponent while utilizing their stronger muscles when executing their slashes and attacks. Toshi, however, developed and perfected a more uncommon reverse grip by holding the Katana with the blade facing down since he preferred the strategy of infighting, fighting up close with his opponents. Although the risk is higher the closer you are to your opponents, the reverse grip allowed Toshi to reverse the direction of his blade more quickly, thus taking advantage of his speed and timing.

He routinely tested his skills on adult men in the village and easily defeated them in friendly battles. The only person he could not beat was his older sister. His sister had grown into a beautiful and strong woman. She loved white camellias and always had one tied in her long black hair. No matter how hard Toshi tried, she always overcame his strength with leverage, and she was consistently two to three moves ahead of him. After all these years, when she trained with Toshi, she would still let go of her submission holds with a smile to make it look like Toshi had escaped on his own. She was the strongest fighter in the village and the best warrior he knew.

To be a Samurai, you needed to live according to Bushido's tenants, the warrior's way. Bushido was a code of conduct of the Samurai which stressed loyalty, duty and honor. However, a few Samurai didn't follow this code and became outcasts of society. They were known as honorless Samurai. These Samurai were fueled by greed and used force to take from those who were weaker than them. Toshi and his sister were told about these honorless Samurai since they were little children and they were warned about one ruthless Samurai in particular, known as the hooded Samurai. The hooded Samurai killed women and children with absolutely no remorse. He was known to decimate and kill off entire villages throughout Japan.

One day when Toshi was 18, he was walking down the path from his village to Shakujii Lake. He was feeling the breeze on his face and enjoying the different colors the fall season brought when he heard screaming from the village. He ran up the path and saw the look of horror on the faces of villagers gathered in the open field in the center of the village. The Cherry Blossom Trees surrounding the field were bare this time of year and Toshi felt a coldness he had never felt before. As he approached, he could see the feet of someone lying on the floor. The villagers looked at Toshi with fear and terror in their eyes. Toshi, out of breath, saw a lifeless body on the floor, surrounded by blood. He immediately knew who it was. There was a white camellia next to the body. It was his sister.

Across the open field stood an older man wearing a black hood covering his face. Toshi would never forget those icy eyes staring back at him. It was a look devoid of any feeling of humanity. The hooded Samurai's sword had his sister's blood still fresh on its sharp cold blade. Toshi had been training his whole life for this moment. He couldn't contain the anger inside of him, and he had his katana on his waist, ready for him to draw and use.

All the villagers looked at Toshi, waiting to see what his reaction would be, waiting to see him avenge his sister's death and protect their village. Instead of using the hundreds of techniques and combinations he had learned over the years from his father, Toshi stood there, frozen in fear. He knew in his mind that if his sister could not defeat this Samurai, there was no way he would be able to.

He watched in a trance as the hooded Samurai demanded the grains the villagers had saved up for the upcoming winter. It wasn't until Toshi heard the screams of his father and mother, now weeping next to their daughter, that Toshi came back to his senses. He locked eyes with his parents and saw something that made his heart sink. He saw the look of disappointment in their eyes. At that moment, filled with shame, grief and despair, Toshi turned around and ran. He would not return to Shakujii Village for 20 years.

The 7 years following his sister's death were dark for Toshi. He spent years traveling Japan motivated by revenge, testing and honing his skills with no emotion against countless opponents. In every battle, he thought about his sister and was determined to hunt down and kill as many honorless Samurai as possible so nobody would have to experience the pain and loss he felt. He never froze again in all his battles and killed without hesitation. He was decisive in all his techniques with no wasted movements. Toshi was considered a hero to villagers all over the country, and by the time he was 25 years old, he was already known as the most feared and respected Samurai in all of Japan.

Toshi had achieved so much at such a young age but was easily distracted and never satisfied. After each victory, he was already thinking and planning for his next battle. No matter how many opponents he defeated, he couldn't explain nor understand a deep feeling of insecurity and unfulfillment. No matter what he accomplished, Toshi felt an emptiness inside of him that could not be filled.

When Toshi was 25 years old, he married a loving wife named Michiyo. She had long brown hair with enchanting brown eyes so deep that Toshi saw his whole life reflected in them. Toshi felt loved, safe and secure whenever he was with her. Their connection was instant as if Toshi's soul had finally found someone it had been searching for over many lifetimes. She complimented Toshi perfectly and was the first person in his life who he could be completely himself around. There was nobody more perfect than her to be his partner for life. Toshi learned from Michiyo that a strong partnership doesn't always have 2 strong people at the same time. It is 2 partners who take turns being strong for each other when the other feels weak.

Over the next 14 years, Toshi and Michiyo had five children, 4 boys and one little girl. His 4 boys were strong yet compassionate and full of laughter. His daughter being the youngest and having to deal with 4 older brothers, was tough and determined. Toshi could already see his sister in his daughter's eyes.

Toshi had fame, success, a loving family and everything in life one can only dream of. He was grateful for everything he was given, but the feeling of emptiness never went away. Throughout the years, Toshi often wondered if fighting the hooded Samurai and getting revenge for his sister was the only way for him to fill the void he was feeling. He knew he eventually had to confront and see those ice-cold eyes again, but everything inside of him told him he was not ready yet.

CHAPTER 2

The Perfect Katana

On Toshi's 39th birthday, he received a message from his mother that his father was dying and needed to see him. Toshi returned to his village for the first time in over 20 years. The village was full of people welcoming him home as they had all heard about his victorious battles throughout Japan. Instead of feeling proud of his achievements, Toshi felt anxiety and embarrassment. No matter how much he had accomplished, the only thing he could think about now that he was back home was how he did nothing the day his sister was killed.

Wanting to be alone, Toshi walked to the open field and stood at the location where his sister lay years ago. For a moment, he froze and could not move. The feelings he had as an 18-year-old full of fear and insecurity came rushing back to him. Despite being victorious in over

200 battles and being the most respected Samurai in Japan, for that moment, he was a child again, feeling ashamed, scared and all alone.

Toshi wanted nothing more than to run away again, but he knew he had to see his father. He walked into his home and saw his father lying on a futon, a traditional Japanese sleeping pad stuffed with cotton on the floor. His father looked smaller than Toshi remembered.

"Father, I am home. I'm sorry for not coming back for so many years. I was full of shame, and I didn't want to come home until I knew I could make you proud," said Toshi as he got on his knees in front of the futon, looking at the tatami floor.

In a soft voice, his father said, "Your mother and I have been waiting for you to come home for years but what matters is you are home now. I have been so happy to hear about all your victories over the years. Your sister would have been so proud of you."

The thought of his sister being proud of him brought tears to Toshi's eyes, but he quickly stopped himself from crying as he didn't want to show any weakness.

His father motioned to a dark cabinet covered in dust and said to his wife, "Please bring it to me." Toshi's mother opened the cabinet and brought out an object wrapped in a soft red and blue silk cloth. She placed the object on her husband's lap.

Toshi's father slowly unwrapped the cloth and revealed a Katana inside. The perfection of this Katana was one that Toshi had never seen before. It had a bluish tinge on the blade of the sword. The handle was made of gold with a carving of a dragon on it and at the point where the handle met the blade was Japanese writing engraved in the steel that read, "Power of 7" with 7 circles surrounding it.

Toshi's father placed the Katana in Toshi's hands and for a moment, Toshi could have sworn that he felt the sword vibrate as if it were greeting him. His father let out a deep, rumbling cough and then placed his hand on Toshi's forearm. Toshi felt the warmth from his father and was reminded of the warmth and love he felt when his father would wrap him up in a blanket as a child. A mixed wave of emotions flooded Toshi as he felt sadness and regret for leaving his mother and father alone for all these years when they needed him the most.

In a soft voice, his father said, "Take this Katana. I have been saving it for you. When I was younger, I saved the life of a Master Samurai. In return, he gave me this sword as a gift. He told me that there were 7 Master Samurai that lived in different locations throughout Japan and each of them had knowledge to release blockages of specific energy centers in your body. If one could release the blockages of all 7 energy centers then you would have the ability to become the highest version of yourself and reach your highest potential both in battle and in life."

Toshi couldn't believe what he was hearing as he had heard this story countless times as a child. "Father, are you telling me that the story you told my sister and I when we were kids was actually true?"

Toshi's father coughed uncontrollably. Toshi placed his hand on his father's chest and asked his mother to bring some tea. After drinking some hot tea, his father's cough subsided. His father replied in a weak voice, "Yes. The story was true. Whenever you are ready, the Master Samurai who gave me this katana lives in the Arisugawa forest in the Minato province. He can teach you to unlock your first energy center, and once you are successful, he will tell you where to find the second Master."

With one hand on his father's chest and the other hand clutching the Katana, Toshi said, "Father, I will not leave you and mother again."

Toshi's father replied, "Toshi, you do not have to stay with us. We do not blame you for leaving us when you did. Everyone has their own path in life. I lived a complete and fulfilling life. I am so grateful for this moment that I can see the man you have grown to be." His father paused. Toshi couldn't be sure whether he saw tears in his father's eyes. His father continued, "Toshi, your mom and I are so proud of you. We have always been proud of you."

A few days later, Toshi's father passed away.

"Mother, I want to stay with you and take care of you," said Toshi.

His mother responded with a smile, "Do I look like someone that needs to be taken care of? I am stronger than you know. I'm the one who was holding our home together during the years you were gone."

Toshi looked at his mom. "I am so sorry I've been gone all these years."

His mother continued, "You are about to embark on a journey that will change your life. I fully support you. Just promise that when your journey is over, you will bring your wife and children home to meet me."

Toshi gave his mother a deep bow and promised he would return someday.

"Make sure you stay warm and don't sleep too late," she yelled as he said his goodbyes and left the village.

On the way to Arisugawa forest, Toshi couldn't contain his excitement. He had dreamed about Master Samurai and energy centers as a child, and he couldn't believe he would actually meet them and learn the secrets. Toshi knew he would have to learn to release the blockages from all 7 of his energy centers to become the highest version of himself and if he wanted to have a chance of defeating the hooded Samurai someday.

Arisugawa forest had cascading hills, valleys and numerous ponds filled with beautiful Koi fish. At the base of the forest was a heavily wooded area with streams and waterfalls. The forest inhabited the world's tallest cedar tree said to be over 3,000 years old.

As Toshi entered Arisugawa forest, the sunlight above was blocked out by the dense canopy of leaves from the trees overhead, leaving only thin rays of light to pass through and reach the forest ground. He could hear the sounds of birds chirping and the endless buzzing sound of cicadas, insects with short, stout bodies and clear membrane wings. The deeper into the forest he reached, the lighter and more relaxed he seemed to feel.

After what felt like hours, Toshi reached steps that appeared to be built into the hillside. He felt inexplicable energy pulling him up the stairs. When Toshi reached the top of the steps, he saw an old shack made of wood. As Toshi stood there gasping for air, he heard a voice that said, "I see you brought the sword I gave your father."

Toshi was startled as he looked around to see where the voice was coming from. Behind him stood an old bald Samurai wearing a black silk kimono with loose-fitting hakama pants.

"Hello," said Toshi. "Are you the Master Samurai my father told me about?"

"I am. I have been waiting a long time for you. I knew you would eventually show up," replied the Master.

"Waiting for me?" asked Toshi with a surprised look.

"Yes, your father was a great Samurai. He saved my life in a battle. If it were not for him, I would have been killed by a group of honorless Samurai years ago."

Toshi didn't believe what he had heard. "You must be mistaken. My father was a great battle strategist but never a great fighter."

The Master shook his bald head and said, "Your father was one of the best fighters of his time and respected by many. He could have been a personal bodyguard to the Shogun himself, but your father quit fighting and vowed never to kill another human being after you and your sister were born. He wanted to dedicate his life to teaching you both everything he knew because he loved you so much."

Toshi couldn't believe what he was hearing. "I can't believe my father was a great fighter. He never mentioned that to me."

The Master shook his head. "Your father was always so humble. Most of the battle strategies that are taught to young Samurai were developed by your father from his own battle experiences."

The Master continued, "It's great to finally meet you. I have heard about your battle victories all over Japan. The stories I have heard about you reminded me of the stories about your father when he was your age. After he saved my life, I gave him the sword that you now carry on the side of your waist and told him that if he ever wanted to become the highest version of himself and reach his fullest potential in life, to come to me. I told him I would teach him the secrets to releasing the blockages of his energy centers so he could find lasting peace and fulfillment. Your father was a little younger than you when he came to see me for his lesson."

Toshi felt a warmth overcome his body as he imagined his father making the journey to change his life as he was about to do.

The Master said, "He had won hundreds of battles and had everything in life he ever wanted, but he too felt unfulfilled. Often, the people who have accomplished most in life feel the most empty and unfulfilled inside, so he sought to learn the principles of the Power of 7."

Toshi looked off into the distance and saw the sun's warm glow descend below the canopy of the trees. "Did my father learn from all 7 of the Master Samurai?"

The Master smiled and replied, "Yes. He learned the Power of 7 and was able to release the blockages of his 7 energy centers. He successfully achieved his fullest potential and went on to live a fulfilling life."

Toshi couldn't help but be filled with emotion. "He gave up his dreams to teach my sister and I, but my sister was killed in battle, and I let him down when I was too afraid to fight the hooded Samurai."

The Master, with a warm smile, said, "On the contrary. He lived his life fulfilling his dreams and passion of imparting his knowledge and experience to you and your sister. You will learn later when you learn to release the blockage in your throat, your 5th Energy Center, about the effect following your passions will have in allowing you to reach your fullest potential. Your father was so proud of you, and he would have been even more proud to know that you are embarking on the journey, like him, to learn the principles of the Power of 7. Are you ready to embark on this journey to reach your supreme destiny and become the highest version of yourself?"

There was a look of excitement and hope in Toshi's eyes. "I am ready."

CHAPTER 3

The Master of Letting Go

"When you surrender and let go of the past, you allow yourself to be fully alive in the present moment."

-The 4 Agreements by Don Miguel Ruiz

The Master began the lesson early the next morning. "The human body contains 7 major energy centers. When they are all open, you are functioning at the highest levels physically, mentally, emotionally and spiritually."

The Master explained, "The moment we are born, all 7 of these energy centers are open. That's why you see very young children love and laugh completely and express all their emotions freely. However, as the child grows, the energy centers get blocked by limitations and expectations placed on them by their environment, their parents and eventually themselves. They begin comparing themselves with others and are taught they are insignificant, not attractive, unworthy, sinful and unsafe. As the child grows, they begin to believe these lies, and they forget how beautiful, strong, brave, safe, loved, perfect and complete they are. That is why the Power of 7 is so important. When you learn the principles of the Power of 7 and are able to slowly release the blockages of all your energy centers, your soul will begin to remember its true essence."

> *"We are not human beings having a spiritual experience, but we are spiritual beings having a human experience."*
> **–Pierre Teilhard de Chardin**

The Master added, "When you release the blockages of all your energy centers, you will remember that we are all spiritual beings and what life is about. You will learn more about our spiritual connection to God, to the Universe, to Source, and you will learn about your Supreme Destiny when you meet the final Master Samurai who will teach you how to release the blockage of your crown."

The Master continued, "The first step to reaching your fullest potential is to clear the blockage in your first energy center located at the base of your spine. When you release this energy center, you can achieve your highest potential in your mental health. No matter how much success you achieve, no matter how much physical wealth you accumulate, no matter how much love you receive from others, you will not feel fully safe and secure unless you clear the blockage in this first energy center. This is the energy center that I will be focusing on."

Toshi sat in front of the Master. He could feel the warmth of the sun as it appeared above the canopy of trees in the distance. "How do you clear the blockage in the first energy center at the base of your spine?"

"You have to meditate and focus all your energy on letting go of everything in your life that no longer serves you," said the Master. "There are many different types of meditation. There is Zen, Vipassana, Mantra, Transcendental and so on."

"Can you tell me a little bit more about these different types of meditation," asked Toshi.

The Master nodded. "I will give you a brief overview of some of the different types. Zen meditation is rooted in the Buddhist tradition where one usually sits in a crossed legged position and focuses their attention inward by focusing on the breath to remain and be mindful of the here and now. Vipassana meditation is also rooted in the Buddhist tradition and involves sitting quietly and observing your thoughts and emotions as they are without judging or dwelling on them while focusing on your breath. Mantra meditation involves sitting and speaking, chanting, whispering or repeating a syllable, word or phrase repeatedly as a tool to help you clear your mind and be present in the moment. Transcendental meditation is similar to Mantra meditation with the only difference being in Transcendental meditation, the repeated mantra is a meaningless sound."

The Master continued, "Each meditation practice has countless and proven benefits to help one clear their mind and reach their highest potential. There is no right or wrong way to meditate and there is not one practice which is better than the others. You just have to find the practice that you connect with the most. Regardless of which meditation practice you prefer, the common theme of most meditation practices is to sit quietly and focus on your breath as a way to clear your mind. In order to clear the blockage in your first energy center, you must have a specific intention while you are meditating."

Toshi looked intrigued. "What is the specific intention we need to be meditating on?"

Past Trauma

"Trauma blocks love, but love heals Trauma"

The Master, with perfect posture, stood in front of Toshi with his hands linked behind his back. In a gentle but firm voice, the Master said, "To release the blockages in your first energy center and feel truly safe and secure, you must meditate to clear your mind, and once your mind is clear, you must focus on a specific intention of letting go of past trauma. Everyone in life has experienced some form of past trauma, whether big or small. Oftentimes, this trauma occurred when you were younger and may even be an event you no longer remember or have blocked from your memory. If past trauma is not addressed and released, any external stimuli that subconsciously reminds you of the traumatic event may trigger you to feel trauma symptoms as an adult, such as anxiety, insecurity, depression, sadness or anger."

Toshi sat still and listened intently to the Master. "Can you tell me more about how past trauma can affect our daily lives as an adult?"

1. Understanding Triggers

The Master explained, "Our brain is designed to keep us safe. When you are faced with a perceived threat, your Sympathetic Nervous System activates the fight, flight or freeze response by releasing stress hormones into your body, such as adrenaline and cortisol which causes your pupils to narrow, increases your heart rate and increases blood flow to the muscles. This is an instinctual response in the face of perceived danger that prepares your body to either fight or run away. When a threat seems impossible to fight off or escape, your nervous system enters the freeze or shutdown state. After the threat is over, our Parasympathetic Nervous System restores our body to a state of calm and safety."

"Let me give you an example of this," said the Master. "If you were in the forest and you came face to face with a bear, your nervous system would release stress hormones into your body preparing your body to either fight or run away. If you were then cornered by the bear and it seemed impossible to escape, your nervous system may then cause your body to freeze up and shut down. These instinctual responses are beneficial to us because they optimize and prepare our bodies to respond to danger."

"That is amazing how our body works," said Toshi.

"It really is," said the Master. "Our body is constantly trying to protect us, but sometimes, it tries to protect us from harm that isn't there which can have a negative effect on our daily lives. When you experience a traumatic event in your life, sometimes your brain will pair something that is actually safe with that trauma. When a neutral stimulus gets paired with a physiological reaction, such as the fight, flight or freeze response, we call that a trigger."

Toshi looked confused. "I've never heard of a trigger before. Can you give me an example of this?"

The Master responded, "Yes of course. A basic example would be a child who was bit by a dog when she was young. This traumatic event may cause the child to grow up fearing dogs even though most dogs are not dangerous or harmful. If that fear is not addressed, anytime the child sees a dog, her Sympathetic Nervous System will activate her fight, flight or freeze response. When that child grows up to be an adult and sees a Shiba Inu, a Japanese hunting dog, she is triggered and may feel trauma symptoms, such as fear and anxiety no matter how many times she is told the dog is friendly and not aggressive."

"That is so interesting that we can be triggered by something that is not dangerous just because of a negative or traumatic experience we had in the past," said Toshi.

"It really is," replied the Master. "When you are triggered by a safe event that has been paired with some past trauma, your body activates your fight, flight or freeze response causing you to feel trauma symptoms I mentioned earlier such as anxiety and depression even though you are not in any danger. Since anxiety, insecurity and depression are uncomfortable, the most common response to the safe event that is triggering you is to avoid or ignore it. Sometimes, if the past trauma was severe, you may respond to the triggering event by freezing or shutting down. Responding to triggers by avoiding them or shutting down can take the form of being hyper focused on distractions, keeping yourself overly busy, overeating to feel better about yourself or relying on substances such as alcohol or narcotics to numb your feelings. However, every time you avoid a trigger or allow yourself to shut down, it reinforces your brain to avoid a stimulus that is actually safe, and it increases your anxiety, insecurity and depression around that stimulus."

The Master continued, "So in the example I just gave you, since she feels fear and anxiety around dogs, the most common response is for her to do everything she can to avoid dogs. The problem is, every time she avoids dogs, it reinforces her belief that dogs are dangerous and increases her fear and anxiety around dogs. What the adult needs to understand is that the fear and anxiety is not caused by the Shiba Inu or seeing the Shiba Inu. Instead, those trauma symptoms are caused by remnants of the negative energy felt from being bit by the dog as a child that has not been resolved, let go and released. The remnants of unresolved energy caused by the traumatic event must be addressed, let go and released for her to begin healing from her current fear."

The Master paused for a moment to make sure Toshi was following. The Master added, "When you are exposed to extreme or recurring fear or trauma, it takes your body longer to return to a state of calm and your brain will remember that trauma on a subconscious level and pair anything associated with that trauma with the fight, flight or freeze response. When it comes to trauma, your body is not only reacting to the present moment's sense of danger but the memory of past danger that has been stored in your nervous system."

"Can you give me an example of recurring trauma?" asked Toshi.

"Certainly," replied the Master. "Think of a child who grew up in a household where her parents did not provide the child with love and attention and instead were constantly yelling and physically abusive to one another. That child's Sympathetic Nervous System was constantly activated, and her body was always in a fight, flight or freeze response mode. Since the child had to constantly witness her parent's abuse, her Parasympathetic Nervous System could not allow her to feel safe and secure like a child who grew up in a more stable environment. Her brain on a subconscious level remembers the ongoing fear and trauma she experienced as a child and pairs anything associated with that trauma with the fight, flight or freeze response. When that child grows up to be an adult, even the smallest confrontation, disagreement or even loud noise may remind her of the past trauma and trigger her to feel trauma symptoms, such as anxiety, insecurity, depression, sadness or anger. She may have a normal disagreement with a partner or friend and instead of communicating and using that disagreement to grow, she may feel trauma symptoms causing her to avoid the confrontation and shut down, further reinforcing her anxiety and fear around those normal situations."

"How can one learn to not be triggered by situations that are actually safe?" asked Toshi.

2. Unpairing Triggers to Past Trauma

"What we resist, persists. Embrace it and it will resolve."
−Carl Jung

The Master answered, "You must break the pairing of the neutral stimulus or trigger with the past trauma. When an event occurs that causes you to feel trauma symptoms such as anxiety, insecurity, depression, sadness or anger, the first step is to understand and accept that you are being triggered and embrace the situation instead of resisting and avoiding it. When you understand that you are being triggered, you should first ask yourself whether the event or situation that is triggering you is actually dangerous. If the event or situation is not dangerous, you must break the pairing of that event with your past trauma by gradually exposing yourself to that safe situation instead of avoiding it. When you gradually expose yourself to that safe situation and your body realizes that you are not harmed by it, your mind begins to break the pairing of that safe situation with your past trauma and stops releasing stress hormones into your body that activates your fight, flight or freeze response when you are triggered."

Toshi thought about this and asked, "So in the example of the adult feeling trauma symptoms when experiencing arguments, disagreements or loud noise, she needs to first understand that it's not the disagreements with her partner or friends that are triggering her trauma symptoms but her traumatic experiences she experienced as a child?"

"Exactly," replied the Master.

Toshi thought for a moment. "She needs to ask herself if disagreements with her partner or friends are actually dangerous? Since they are not dangerous, should she gradually expose herself to those situations instead of avoiding them to unpair the trigger with her past trauma?"

"Yes," said the Master.

"Between stimulus and response there is a space. In that space is our power to choose our response. In our response lies our growth and our freedom."
–Victor Frankl, Holocaust Survivor

The Master continued, "When you are triggered, you have the power to choose whether you will avoid the situation that is triggering you or embrace it to try and grow. When you gradually expose yourself to safe situations that are triggering you, although uncomfortable at first, it will ultimately allow your mind to break the pairing of those safe situations with your past trauma. You must learn that it is not the current situation that is triggering those traumatic symptoms, but the traumatic event you experienced as a child that must be let go. If that past traumatic event is not healed and if that negative energy associated with that past event is not let go, then as an adult, you will have endless situations that will cause you to have trauma symptoms because you are reacting unsuccessfully to the current situation instead of healing the root cause. This prevents us from living to our fullest potential because we are always reacting to something out of our control."

Toshi understood the lesson and asked, "Master, can you teach me how to address, let go and release these past traumatic experiences?"

Letting Go of Past Trauma

1. Healing Your Inner Child

The Master answered, "One way to release the unresolved energy caused by traumatic events when you were younger is to work on healing your inner child."

"How do I do that," asked Toshi.

The Master responded. "That's where meditation comes in. When you meditate, you must focus and contemplate what your inner child needs from you in order to heal. Try to remember the traumatic event that occurred in your life. A lot of times, we block out the traumatic events of our childhood and don't want to think or relive those moments. To truly heal your inner child, it is important to take yourself back to those traumatic events. Imagine yourself in that situation again. What were you feeling? What were you thinking? What were you scared of? Then ask yourself what your inner child would have needed and wanted in that moment to feel safe and secure."

The Master continued, "Imagine what you would say to yourself as a little child. Would you say, don't be afraid? You are loved and worthy of love? You are strong? I am proud of you? You have nothing to be afraid of because I will protect you? The way you connect with your inner child is by using your strong adult voice that you have now in situations where back then, you had no other choice but to feel scared, alone, powerless and insecure. If you do this often and consistently, your inner child will eventually be convinced that it has nothing to be afraid of. When you can heal the insecurity and fears of your inner child, you are treating the root cause, and you will therefore see positive effects in your adult life as there will be fewer situations that will trigger you causing unnecessary trauma symptoms."

Toshi took a deep breath as he remembered standing in the open field when his sister was killed by the hooded samurai. He remembered how scared, powerless and alone he felt. Toshi thought about how as an adult, he would often be triggered by situations that made him feel powerless or scared. Those situations would always make him feel anxiety, and he would lash out in anger. Toshi realized that the root cause of his anxiety was that he never healed and released the negative energy associated with his sister's death.

The Master continued, "Even though there are times when we feel like a child again when we are triggered, we need to remind ourselves that we are now adults and have more resources to fight and protect ourselves. When we are triggered, you must ask yourself, what is it that is triggering you right now? Why are you being triggered by this external stimulus? When you begin feeling the trauma symptoms such as insecurity, anger or depression, you need to ask yourself, what is it you really want right now to feel safe, secure and loved? What is it you really need right now to feel safe, secure and loved? It is in those moments when you must give yourself the love, attention and security that you didn't receive as a child. When we feel safe in the face of a trigger, our brain no longer releases hormones to activate our Sympathetic Nervous System preparing our body to fight, flight or freeze. Instead, our brain activates our Parasympathetic Nervous system allowing our body to return to a state of security and connection."

Toshi said, "Any time there was an event that caused me to feel sad, angry, depressed or alone, I always thought it was the event that was making me feel that way. That's why it was so hard for me to feel better in those situations. I never knew that those negative feelings were caused by traumatic events I experienced as a child that I needed to heal and let go of."

The Master replied, "Once you can let go of past trauma, you can begin to release the blockage of your first energy center and feel truly safe and secure."

2. Negative Experiences, Negative Thought Patterns & Limiting Beliefs

The Master sat down next to Toshi and looked compassionately into his eyes. "You must also let go of all negative experiences, negative thought patterns and limiting beliefs about yourself. Everyone has negative experiences in life. It is so important that you not internalize your past failures or negative experiences, and you must not let them define who you are. Past failures are just there to point your life in a different direction. You must forgive the past because what matters is now, this moment and what you decide to do with it."

Toshi said, "There are negative experiences I have had in the past that made me feel unworthy. I am always questioning whether I am good enough to win my next battle or good enough as a son, father and husband. I think that is why I am always distracted and thinking about my next battle. I feel I am only worthy if I constantly win and succeed."

The Master said, "Let go of all your limiting beliefs about yourself. Let go of thoughts that you can't accomplish your goals and dreams. Let go of beliefs that you are not good enough. You are so much stronger than you know. There is a purpose for everything that has occurred in your life to bring you to this exact moment. During moments of your greatest despair will often come the greatest lessons and gifts. You must understand that any pain you have experienced in your life happened for you to learn to love yourself unconditionally and not rely on something external to feel loved, worthy or reassured of your self-worth. You will learn more about feeling worthy and self-worth when you meet the 4th Master Samurai who will teach you to release the blockage in your heart, your 4th energy center. You are destined for so much more in life, and once you learn the Power of 7, you will be able to become the highest version of yourself and live life to your fullest potential."

Toshi responded, "How can I let go of these negative thought patterns and limiting beliefs about myself."

The Master paused for a moment and said, "You must constantly remind yourself of all you had to go through and overcome to get to this current point in your life. Forgive yourself and release all the negative feelings and emotions you are carrying about those past experiences. Use your memory of who you were and what you had to endure to be proud of how far you've come. Accept that your darkness is the contrast to your light. It is the obstacles and challenges that you have faced in life that will allow you to use those experiences to have a positive impact on others and for you to truly appreciate what you have and what you will become."

"Even though I have accomplished so much, I have a lot of negative thought patterns and limiting beliefs about myself," said Toshi.

"It's important to take care of your mental health. Let go of all your past trauma, and don't allow yourself to be triggered by safe events that remind you of those traumatic events. It is time to let go of everything in your life that no longer serves you. Release all the negativity," replied the Master.

The Master decided to continue the lesson the next day to give Toshi a chance to reflect on what he had learned. Toshi spent the remainder of the day at the bottom of the steps watching the Koi fish gliding effortlessly and peacefully through the water with nothing holding them back.

Negative People and Toxic Relationships

"Every day, we awake with a certain amount of mental, emotional and physical energy that we spend throughout the day. If we allow our emotions to deplete our energy, we have no energy to change our lives or to give to others."

–Don Miguel Ruiz

1. Negative People

The next morning, Toshi and the Master walked down the steps and down a small path that led to a small waterfall. The water bounced off the rocks below into a crystal-clear Caribbean blue serene pond. As they got closer, Toshi could feel the wet mist on his face, bringing a feeling of nostalgia as the memory of playing in the lake in his village with his sister came to mind.

The Master continued with his lesson. "To release the blockage of your first energy center, you must also let go of negative people. Everything in the world is made up of energy. People are no different. There are people in your life with more positive energy, and there are others with more negative energy. You must conserve and save energy for the people who really matter in your life, including yourself."

Toshi thought about this and said, "Yes, I've noticed that there are some people in my life where I feel drained and tired after I spend time with them. There are others like my wife and kids who always make me feel happy and energetic when I am in their presence."

"That is exactly right," replied the Master. "Be in the presence of positive energy and people who make you feel happy, loved and worthy and stay away from people who make you feel tired, drained or insecure. You must cut the cord between you and people who take away your energy. Sometimes, for you to reach your fullest potential, this means you might also have to stay away from some family members no matter how much you want to love and help them. You have to learn that it is never your responsibility to take somebody else from where they are to where they need to be. You need to work on yourself first, and when you get to that point, you can inspire others with the work you did, and hopefully, you will see them working on improving themselves in the future."

"Do not serve from an empty cup. Fill your own cup first, then serve from the overflow."

2. Toxic Relationships

"You are not meant to jump in water to save someone from drowning if you can't swim yourself. Instead, send them love and light from a distance."
–Kristine Ovsepian, Journeys to Heal

The Master continued, "You must also let go of toxic relationships in your life. You must go where the love is and leave where it isn't. You should never have to convince someone to love you or give someone else the power to determine your worth. You should never have to stay in a relationship where you feel unhappy, unloved, unsafe and insecure. Sometimes, the purest way of saying I love you is to say goodbye."

The Master continued, "There is a famous Kabuki play where the lead actor rushes over to his love interest and says to her in one of the most romantic scenes of all time, "You Complete Me." The problem with the belief someone or something else can complete you implies that you are not complete, to begin with. Some people tell themselves that they would feel complete if they had more money. Others tell themselves that meeting someone who could make them feel happy or loved would complete them. When we give the power to something external to make us feel complete when they provide us with something we are missing, such as attention, love or validation, then we also give them the power to make us feel incomplete when they take it away. The truth you have to understand is that you don't need validation, acceptance or love from an outside source because you are already undeniably and eternally complete."

"I understand," said Toshi. "There is a lot in my life I need to let go of that no longer serves me. I need to protect my energy more and conserve it so I can use it to become the highest version of myself and give it to people who are important to me."

The Power of the Rising Sun

Toshi asked, "Do you have any guidance on how I can improve my meditation practice?"

The Master replied, "When you meditate, you should find a time to yourself where you can be apart from all your daily distractions and be present in the moment. You can accomplish this by focusing on your breath. Every time you focus on your breath, you activate your Parasympathetic Nervous System and allow your body to return to calm. When your body and mind are calm, you can focus on healing and letting go of things that no longer serve you. You can meditate any time of the day to get positive benefits, but when you meditate early in the morning when the sun rises, you get the most profound effect. Everything in the world is made up of energy; the energy is strongest and most positive when the sun rises. Your mind is also at its optimum level and most creative when you wake up early before you are bombarded with the distractions of daily life. Getting enough sleep for your brain and body to repair, restore and reenergize is equally as important as waking up when the sun rises. Sleeping and waking up early will put you in the best position to get the most out of your meditation to clear the blockage in your first energy center."

Toshi responded, "I want to begin waking up as the sun rises. Usually, when I wake up, my children are already awake, and I give them all my attention. Other times, I already have to focus on all my obligations for that day by the time I wake up. It would be nice to wake up early enough so I can have time to focus and contemplate on myself and meditate on letting go of things in my life that no longer serve me. I would love to have time to myself before I am bombarded with the obligations and distractions of daily life."

The Master replied, "That is the benefit of waking up as the sun rises. When you begin doing that consistently, you will see your creativity flourish and experience positive impacts on every other part of your life."

"Rising at 5 AM truly is the mother of all routines. The 5 AM club is the one behavior that raises every other human behavior."
–Robin Sharma

The Master concluded the day's lesson. "I think this is enough for today. You have traveled a long way, and you have a long journey ahead to learn the remaining principles of the Power of 7."

Toshi woke up the next morning while it was still dark outside. The Master was already awake and preparing a morning tea, brewing a mixture of some roots and leaves from the trees found locally in Arisugawa forest. Toshi drank the bitter tea and sat underneath the world's tallest cedar tree, where he closed his eyes and meditated. As the sun rose, Toshi could hear the forest come alive with birds chirping and cicadas buzzing. He heard the waterfall nearby and felt the energy from the rising sun surge through his body. Toshi closed his eyes, cleared his mind and focused on his breath.

Suddenly, Toshi was transported to a familiar place. He was back home in Shakujii village. He saw villagers gathering around an individual lying on the floor. Toshi remembered this scene vividly. It was the day his sister was killed by the hooded Samurai. Toshi wasn't sure at this moment if he was transported back in time, if he was hallucinating or dreaming. He saw his younger self all alone with a look of terror and fear in his eyes as he stood next to his sister lying on the ground. He remembered that all his younger self wanted at that moment was to be comforted and told that he was safe. Toshi remembered how sad and alone he felt. For the first time, Toshi cried uncontrollably. He understood that showing emotions was not a sign of weakness but a sign of strength because it demonstrated he was comfortable with his relationship with himself. He knew crying would allow him to release some of the negative energy stored inside of him he had kept inside for all these years from the traumatic events of his past.

Toshi walked up to his younger self and hugged him tightly. Toshi said, "I am older and stronger now. I will always protect you. You are safe. You are not alone. You are loved. I am so proud of you" As he said these words, something unexpected happened. For the first time in Toshi's life, he felt safe, secure and loved.

When Toshi opened his eyes, he saw the Master standing in front of him with kindness and warmth in his eyes. The Master said, "Congratulations. You have just begun to release the blockage in your first energy center."

CHAPTER 4

The Architect and The Cherry Blossom

"Real generosity toward the future consists in giving all to what is present."

–Albert Camus

The Master told Toshi that to learn to release the blockage in his second energy center, he needed to travel to the bronze statue known as Hachiko in the village of Shibuya. There he would meet the second Master Samurai.

The story of Hachiko was known throughout Japan as a symbol of love, devotion and loyalty. In a small village in Shibuya, a bronze statue of an Akita dog was constructed. The statue was built to honor the story of a dog named Hachiko so devoted to his Master he waited for him each day in the village. After the Master passed away, Hachiko continued to wait every day in the middle of the village for 9 years until she also passed.

It didn't take too long for Toshi to arrive at Shibuya village. He was still excited about all he had learned from the first Master Samurai. When he reached the statue of Hachiko, he was met by a man wearing a tailored, blue pin-striped suit with a perfectly folded white pocket square placed in his chest pocket. The man bowed to Toshi.

Toshi spoke first. "I am here to see the second Master Samurai to learn how to release the blockages of my second energy center."

The man replied, "Welcome. I am the second Master Samurai."

Toshi looked confused, "I'm sorry, but you don't look like a Master Samurai."

The man laughed, "After I learned the principles of the Power of 7, I decided to follow my passions and became an architect. I designed and came up with the idea for the Hachiko statue."

Toshi bowed 90 degrees to the architect to show his deep respect and said, "I am so sorry for my rudeness. It is an honor to meet you."

The Architect smiled at Toshi's show of respect. "Would you like to rest first, or would you like to begin your lesson?"

"I didn't have to travel too far to get here. I am ready to begin if that is ok with you," said Toshi.

The Pot of Gold

"We are so focused on the pot of gold at the end of the rainbow that we fail to see the gold sprinkled throughout the journey."

The Architect began his lesson. "The second step to reaching your fullest potential and finding peace and lasting fulfillment is to clear the blockage in your second energy center located in an area below your navel. In a time where distractions surround you from the moment you wake up to the time you go to bed, you are constantly prevented from being present and grateful. All the distractions in your life cause blockages in your second energy center, which needs to be released. When you are constantly distracted and not appreciating the small and big things in your life, you are prevented from receiving all the positive energy and abundance you are destined to receive. To reach your fullest potential, you must clear your mind and be present and grateful for even the little things in your life. When used properly, your mind is a powerful tool for making all your desires, dreams and goals come true. You will learn more about the secret to using the power of your mind to manifest whatever you want in your life when you later learn to release the blockage in the area on your forehead between your eyes, your 6th energy center."

The Architect continued, "The ego is always obsessed with the future and planning for the future because it believes that if it doesn't keep on obsessing about it, something bad will happen when the opposite is true. When you stop obsessing about the future and things outside of your control, you will see all the wonderful and positive things happening right now. Everyone is always working so hard to reach the pot of gold at the end of the rainbow they forget to enjoy the journey there. If they focus more on the moment and be present during each step, they will realize that the gold is sprinkled throughout the journey."

The Architect looked at Toshi. "Have you ever experienced going through your day and then not really remembering details about what you did during that day? As if you were just going through the motions?"

"Yes," replied Toshi. "Sometimes when I am with my children, I am so distracted by my thoughts of what I want to accomplish in the future that I don't even know what they have said to me. I want to be more present when I am with them, but I don't know how. I have so much going on in my mind. When they were young, all I could think about was how I couldn't wait until they were older so I wouldn't have to worry about them as much. Now that they are older, I wish I was more present when they were younger because time seems to be flying by so fast and there are so many moments that I missed. Instead of being present and enjoying my time when I was with them, I was constantly thinking, worrying about and planning for the future."

"That is totally understandable," said the Architect. "Ambitious individuals often times have a lot going on in their mind. When your mind is full of distractions though, it blocks your second energy center because it prevents you from being fully present and grateful in the moment and therefore prevents you from receiving all the abundance that is out in the world for you. Don't get me wrong, it is perfectly fine and also a necessity to be ambitious and constantly think about how to improve yourself, which you will learn more about when you meet the 3rd Master Samurai who will teach you how to release the blockage in your solar plexus, your 3rd energy center. However, there has to be a healthy balance of times when you are focusing and being present and times when you are thinking of the future and improving yourself."

"I definitely want to be more present when I am with my wife, kids and other people I love," said Toshi.

The Architect added, "When you are present and focused on the here and now, you are in tune and in balance with all 5 of your senses. When you are with people you love, it is important to be present and give them your undivided attention."

"I understand," said Toshi. "Can you teach me how to be more present in the moment and block out unwanted distractions?"

1. Ground Yourself

"Certainly," said the Architect. "When you want to be present in the moment, it is important to ground yourself so you can tell your mind that this is an important moment you want to be present for."

Toshi looked confused. "I've never heard of grounding myself. What does that mean."

The Architect continued, "Grounding yourself is the process of balancing your physical, emotional, mental and spiritual state and reconnecting them. One way to do this is to focus on your breath. There are many ways to focus on your breath, but one easy way is to inhale through your nose for 4 seconds and then hold your breath for 4 seconds. Then exhale through your mouth for 4 seconds, then again hold your breath again for 4 seconds, and then repeat the cycle by inhaling through your nose again for 4 seconds. When you do this for a few minutes, it relaxes your body, lowers your heart rate and signals to your mind that it needs to focus on the moment. Anytime you feel stressed or distracted, you can ground yourself with this breathing technique."

"Or anytime I am triggered, which will cause trauma symptoms like anxiety, depression, insecurity, anger or sadness, I can ground myself with this technique, right?" asked Toshi with a proud look on his face.

"Yes!" yelled the Architect. "I see the Master of Arisugawa forest has taught you well."

The Architect continued, "Your breath is the most important tool to ground yourself, which will allow you to feel more present and appreciate the moment. Oftentimes, we are so busy during the day that we forget to breathe properly by taking deep breaths."

2. The Beauty of The Cherry Blossom

"Another way to ground yourself to be more present is to activate all 5 of your senses by 1) Focusing on something you can see at the moment, 2) Focusing on something you can touch or feel, 3) Focusing on something you can taste, 4) Focusing on something you can hear and finally, 5) Focusing on something you can smell. When you use all 5 senses to connect with the moment, you are sending a signal to your mind that this is an important moment that it needs to focus on."

The Architect paused and looked directly into Toshi's eyes and asked, "Do you enjoy looking at Sakura Trees and their beautiful cherry blossoms?"

"Of course," replied Toshi. "We have a field surrounded by beautiful cherry blossom trees that bloom every Spring that my village is famous for."

The Architect had a big smile on his face. "Then you know cherry blossoms only bloom for a week or two. We wait all year impatiently, not knowing when the beautiful blossoms will bloom. Then one day, the cherry blossoms start appearing one by one, and all we can do is start worrying about when the blossoms will start falling. Then, after 1 or 2 weeks, they begin falling off the tree as fast as they appeared. Life is just like cherry blossoms. We wait impatiently for events to happen in the future, and when the event finally happens, instead of appreciating the moment, we are already worrying about the next thing. The next time the cherry blossoms bloom in your village, be sure to pause and appreciate the beauty of every individual blossom and the impermanence of life. Ground yourself and be fully present in the here and now because if you are too busy worrying about the future, it will be time for the blossoms to fall from their trees, and before you know it, the trees will once again be bare."

Toshi promised himself that the next time he saw cherry blossoms in his village, he would ground himself and take the time to be fully present and activate all his senses to truly appreciate the moment. After a pause, Toshi asked, "I now understand how to ground myself and be more present, but there are so many things I worry about for the future that distracts my mind. Do you have any guidance on how to stop worrying about the future?"

"Yes," responded the Architect. "You must remember that the only thing you can control is the present moment. You have no control over the future or any outcome you may desire. So instead of focusing on things you cannot control, focus on giving your all to the here and now, the only moment you have control over. Do not allow yourself to be distracted by things that are not important. Instead, spend some quiet time free from distractions so you can focus on your goals, desires and dreams."

"Quiet time is something I wish I had more of," said Toshi.

The Most Precious Gift

"Time is your most precious gift because you only have a set amount of it. You can make more money, but you can't make more time. When you give someone your time, you are giving them a portion of your life that you will never get back. Your time is your life. That is why the greatest gift you can give someone is your time."
–Rick Warren

The Architect said, "As you learned when you released the blockage of your first energy center, it is important to let go of negative people in your life."

"Yes, I learned that lesson from the Master of Arisugawa Forest," said Toshi.

The Architect smiled. "Equally as important as letting go of negative people in your life is taking care of and treasuring the important people in your life. Loyalty is very important, and once you build a positive bond with someone with positive energy who brings out the best in you, don't break that bond unless it is absolutely necessary. Remember all the people who have helped you along the way and do what you can to repay their kindness and support."

"Should I repay them with money," asked Toshi.

"It doesn't necessarily have to be money," replied the Architect. "You can let them know you are thankful for what they have done for you or tell them of their positive impact on your life. You can even send them positive energy through thoughts or prayers. The best gift you can give someone, though, is to give them your time. For the people important to you, give them your full attention when you are with them. That is how you truly let them know how important they are to you."

"Also, don't forget to thank yourself," said the Architect. "The best gift you can give yourself and your future is to give your all to the present moment."

The Architect asked, "Do you need a break? Is this too much information?"

Toshi replied, "No. I am so honored to learn so much from you. If it is ok with you, I would love for you to continue."

Daily Gratitude

The Architect resumed his teaching. "In addition to being present in the moment, you must practice daily gratitude. Instead of constantly focusing on what you don't have or comparing yourself to people who may have more than you, it is important to recognize and appreciate all the positive things in your life and how they affect you. There are so many people in the world who are in a worse position than you. The things you complain about would be a dream for others. Even when something you perceive as negative happens to you, instead of thinking of it as a problem, think of it as a gift. Instead of thinking of an obstacle you are facing as an end, think of it as a beginning."

Toshi responded, "Can you give me an example of this? Sometimes it's difficult to find a positive lesson when something negative happens to you."

The Architect replied, "When something you perceive as negative happens in your life, you may feel sadness, loss and even pain. For example, if you were in a relationship and your partner suddenly ended the relationship, you may experience many different emotions. You may think about how terrible and selfish your partner is. Or you may think that you won't ever find someone as great as your partner in the future. When something you perceive as negative happens in your life, such as losing something or someone you love, oftentimes it's not just mental or emotional pain you feel but physical pain in your heart and gut. In these situations, people always say that time will heal your wounds, but the truth is time does not heal wounds. It's changing the meaning of the event that causes you pain that will heal your wounds. Although we can't control all the events that happen to us in life, we can control what those events mean to us."

"Can you explain this to me a little more?" asked Toshi.

The Architect continued, "Whenever an event happens in your life that you perceive as negative, you must change the meaning of that event in your mind. Instead of thinking of it as a negative experience, think of what you learned from the event. Think of the event as a positive lesson and why you should be grateful that event happened. When you can change the meaning of a negative event in your mind and find ways to be grateful for it, you can begin to heal."

Toshi asked, "How can a person find something to be grateful for if their partner leaves them?"

The Architect sat there quietly for a moment, then responded. "Of course, it is perfectly acceptable to grieve and take time to feel sadness and loss. However, it's important not to let yourself be engulfed in negativity during those times. If your partner leaves you, instead of viewing it as a negative experience, you can focus on all the lessons you learned from your partner while you were together. Focus on the happy times you had together and be grateful for those moments. Understand that sometimes you don't work out with a certain partner because there is someone more perfect for you out there, and you deserve better. Instead of obsessing about something external or someone else, think of your partner leaving as an opportunity for you to obsess about your own happiness and growth. You can change the meaning of the loss by understanding that negative experiences and disappointments in life can drive you to find yourself spiritually or to focus more on yourself and try to become the best version of yourself that you can be. There is always a lesson to be learned in every experience you have, whether positive or negative. Our mind can only focus on one thing at a time. So, when we are focusing on things we are grateful for, it is impossible to be thinking of anything negative during that time so we can begin to heal. Everything you have gone through in life, including the obstacles, challenges, loss and pain you experienced, guides you to your Supreme Destiny."

"What is my Supreme Destiny?" asked Toshi.

The Architect responded, "You will learn more about your Supreme Destiny when you meet the final Master Samurai."

"I can't wait to learn more about that," said Toshi. "Is there anything else I need to know about practicing daily gratitude?"

The Architect continued, "It's important to have a daily routine to remind yourself of what you are grateful for, especially the small things."

"When is a good time to have this gratitude routine?" asked Toshi.

The Architect responded, "The best time to remind yourself of everything you are grateful for in your life is within the first hour after you wake up in the morning. When you start your day off feeling gratitude, you will shift the energy in your body, and the positive energy it creates will be a magnet for more positivity to come into your life throughout the rest of the day. You will learn more about the power of your mind to bring more of what you want into your life when you meet the 6th Master Samurai who will teach you to release the blockages of your 6th energy center."

Toshi thought about this. "So, when I first wake up in the morning, I should try not to be distracted by or focus on anything negative because that may attract more negativity to me during the day?"

"That's right," said the Architect. "When you first wake up in the morning, focus on the small things you are grateful for in life. Be grateful for everything you have in life, whether it be the shelter to keep you safe, a loving family, your health, food to eat or another day to live. Nothing is too big or too small in your life to be grateful for. At the end of the day, before you go to bed, think back and be grateful for all the little things that happened to you during the day."

Toshi stood there feeling grateful for everything that had happened in his life. He was grateful for the air he was breathing. He was grateful for the love he had from his wife and children. He was even grateful for all his negative experiences because those negative experiences have taught him how to appreciate his positive experiences, and they were all necessary to bring him to this moment in life. Toshi had begun to release the blockage of his second energy center and was ready to meet the 3rd Master Samurai.

CHAPTER 5

The Fisherman with No Regrets

"No Shortcuts, No Excuses, No Regrets"

—**Coach Fred Sava**

After resting for a few days, Toshi traveled to Setagaya Village to meet the 3rd Master Samurai. When Toshi arrived, he asked the villagers if they knew of a Master Samurai who lived nearby. They told Toshi of a Master Samurai who loved to fish at Tama River, a river that ran about 86 miles through Tokyo, with part of it flowing through their village.

Toshi's heart beat faster with excitement since he knew the river was within walking distance. He wondered what lesson he would learn from the 3rd Master Samurai. As Toshi approached Tama River, he saw an older man hunched over on the shore holding a fishing pole. His skin was dark and wrinkled from the sun, but he had an aura of peace surrounding him.

"You must be the 3rd Master Samurai," Toshi said with a bow to show his respect.

"Yes," replied the Fisherman. "You must be here to learn how to clear the blockages of your 3rd energy center located in your solar plexus."

"Yes, I am," said Toshi. "Are you catching any fish? There doesn't appear to be any in the river. Aren't you worried that you are wasting valuable time trying to catch fish in a river with no fish instead of doing something more productive?"

The Fisherman replied, "I never worry about whether I will catch any fish. I never focus on the outcome because that is something I cannot control. I have already prepared as much as I can. All I can control is that I do my best and give all my energy, focus and attention to this moment."

Toshi didn't realize that the lesson on releasing the blockage of his 3rd energy center had already started.

Pride And Confidence

"The Way You Do Anything Is The Way You Do Everything"

"When you release the blockages of your 3rd energy center, you can achieve your highest potential in your physical health," said the Fisherman.

1. Pride In Yourself, Pride In Your Work

The Fisherman continued, "From the moment I wake up in the morning, I make it a habit to focus all my energy on every little thing I'm doing and complete each task with pride and full attention. Although I strive for perfection, perfection is not necessary as long as I do my best. No matter how small the task, such as brushing my teeth, I give it my full attention and do my best. When I make my morning green tea, I am patient and take pride when pouring hot water over the leaves. Even when I am doing a task that I don't look forward to doing, such as cleaning the toilets in my home, I take pride in that task, am fully in the moment and try to complete the task to the best of my ability. The habit of taking pride in doing my best in the small things in life makes it easier to take pride and do my best in the bigger things. I need to know that everything I touch and put out into the world will be something I have put all my effort and attention into."

"I have followed the principles of Bushido my whole life. I value duty, honor, dedication and hard work. I feel that the energy center in my solar plexus may have the least amount of blockages of the 7," said Toshi with a grin.

"You are probably right," said the Fisherman. "Yet, I still feel there is something you can learn from this lesson. You must take pride in everything you do, and to accomplish this, you must be proud of who you are. To have pride in who you are, you must be confident in yourself and your abilities."

"What is the difference between confidence and arrogance?" asked Toshi.

2. Inner Confidence

The Fisherman continued, "Confidence is a feeling of self-assurance that comes from an understanding and appreciation of your abilities and qualities. Someone confident does not have to prove their confidence or show off their abilities to others because they know deep down what their abilities are and what they are capable of. Arrogance is having an exaggerated sense of your importance or abilities. Someone arrogant constantly tries to show off their abilities because they believe they are better than everyone around them."

"I've met many arrogant Samurai in my life," said Toshi. "They always talked about themselves and liked to brag about their achievements and victories. Most were very condescending and nobody liked to be around them. I've noticed that the Samurai who were the best fighters were the ones who had quiet confidence in themselves. The confident ones had pride in their abilities and always showed composure and humility."

"That is right," said the Fisherman. "To have pride in yourself and to take pride in your work, you have to develop that inner confidence in your abilities. Many people live life trying to receive compliments from the people around them," said the Fisherman. "They feel a boost of confidence when their partners say they look nice or when their bosses tell them they are doing a great job. The problem with outside validation is that it is always outside your control. You will always search for outside validation and compliments from others to feel good about yourself and to feel confident about your abilities. You will lose your confidence when you cannot receive compliments from others. That's why it's so important to not rely on outside validation. You must have confidence from within yourself."

"Then what is the key to developing inner confidence," asked Toshi.

The Fisherman responded, "Confidence is not gained by compliments. Confidence is gained by accomplishments and knowing you did your best."

Accomplishments

The Fisherman continued, "To develop your inner confidence in your own abilities, you must seek to continually accomplish your goals. To accomplish goals, you must understand the importance of preparation and work ethic, learn to focus on one task at a time, strive to improve yourself on a daily basis and also remember when to relax."

1. The Secret to the 1%

"We don't rise to the level of our expectations; we fall to the level of our preparation."

The Fisherman resumed, "It is very hard to slack in certain areas in your life and expect to be peak performers in other areas because excellence is not about intensity; it's about consistency. It's easy to perform a hard task temporarily for a day or two, but when you consistently do your best, even in practice, you can expect to do your best when it really matters. To succeed at something, you must prepare diligently and practice consistently. Even when practicing, you have to have pride and do your best. People always think that practice makes perfect, but that is not true. It is perfect practice that makes perfect. It's better to perform a task 10 times perfectly than to perform it 100 times imperfectly."

Toshi nodded in agreement. He thought about the countless hours he spent daily as a child perfecting his techniques in the Art of the Sword.

The Fisherman checked his fishing line and saw he had not caught any fish. With no hesitation or disappointment, he cast his line into the river again. "In life, it is perfectly acceptable to have dreams and goals of being in the best shape physically and achieving physical wealth and success. This is important and necessary to reach your fullest potential in your physical health. However, when you try to reach these goals, you must remember not to neglect your mental, emotional and spiritual health because you need to be functioning at the highest level in all aspects of your life to become the highest version of yourself."

"To achieve your dreams and goals of physical wealth and success, you must have a work ethic where you always do your best. To reach the success that 1% of the people in the world have reached, you have to be prepared to do the difficult things that 99% are unwilling to do. When you practice diligently and consistently, you don't have to be stressed or worried about executing when it really matters because the hard part has already been done. Your work ethic eliminates fear because you already know what you are capable of accomplishing and achieving when the time comes."

"Is that why you don't focus on the outcome?" asked Toshi.

"Exactly," said the Fisherman. No matter how much I stress or worry, I can never control a specific outcome. Instead of trying so hard to control a situation completely out of my control that could lead to unhappiness and unfulfillment, I focus on what I can control: how well I prepare and how hard I work in this present moment. As long as I know I did my best, I will have no regrets. That is why it is so important to take pride in every little thing you do, don't take shortcuts and always do your best to live life with no regrets."

The Fisherman gave an example. "When you are going to be in battle, no matter how much you stress or worry, you can never control the outcome. You cannot control how skilled your opponent is or whether your opponent is having a good or bad day. You cannot control whether you will win or lose the battle because there are so many variables that are out of your control. So why spend so much energy worrying and stressing about things completely out of your control? Instead, you should focus your energy on things in your control, such as how well you prepare and train because the more you sweat in practice, the less you bleed in battle."

Toshi asked, "Do you believe hard work and preparation always lead to success? Or do you believe that there is some luck involved?"

The Fisherman replied, "I don't believe in luck. Luck is when opportunity meets preparation. Once again, you can't control what opportunities come into your life, but you can control how prepared you are. As long as you do your best to prepare yourself, when the opportunity finally comes, you will be ready. The important thing is you have to give your all to your preparation."

Toshi thought about this and said, "I have known many Samurai who were lazy when training. They always told me that when it was time for battle, they would step it up and be able to execute. Unfortunately, they were never successful when it really mattered."

"When it's time to perform, you can't expect to rise to the level of your expectations when you have never performed well in practice," said the Fisherman. "Instead, you will always fall to the level of your preparation."

Toshi looked deep in thought. He could hear the river flowing past his feet. "I like to think that I always do my best. Sometimes though, it's hard for me to focus on one task because I have so much going on at the same time. Oftentimes, when I am training Martial Arts or trying to concentrate on battle strategy, my children are running around and asking me to play with them."

2. Be A Laser, Not A Lightbulb

"This is a very important lesson for you Toshi," said the Fisherman. "We are living in a time where there are constant distractions in our lives. We are constantly trying to complete multiple tasks at once. The problem is when we try to complete multiple tasks at once, we are giving none of those tasks our full energy and attention. If we are giving none of those tasks our full energy and attention then we are not doing any of those tasks to the best of our ability. When you are trying to complete multiple tasks at once, you are in essence taking a shortcut because you are trying to get all the tasks done as quickly as possible. When you take shortcuts, you will not achieve the best possible outcome."

"I always thought it was better to get more accomplished at one time by doing multiple tasks at once," said Toshi.

The Fisherman responded, "When you are trying to train Martial Arts and your children are wanting to play with you, do you feel like you are able to train at a high level?"

"No," said Toshi.

"Why not?" asked the Fisherman.

"Because I am not completely focused on training because I feel guilty for not spending time and playing with my children," said Toshi.

"Ok, so when you are trying to train and your children want to play with you, do you feel like you are able to be present with your children and appreciate that time with them?" asked the Fisherman.

"No," said Toshi.

The Fisherman asked again, "Why not?"

Toshi responded, "I can't fully appreciate the moments I have with my children because in the back of my head, I feel like I should be training."

"Exactly," said the Fisherman. "When you try to focus your attention and energy on too many tasks at once, you end up performing none of those tasks well. Instead, focus on one task at a time. When it's time to play with your children, put all your energy into that moment, give them your undivided attention and don't think of any other distractions. When it's time for you to train, put all your energy and focus into that moment."

"That makes sense," said Toshi. "I will definitely try to focus on one task at a time."

"Do you know the difference between a light bulb and a laser?" asked the Fisherman.

Toshi responded, "A light bulb lights up a room and a laser cuts through anything in its way."

"Yes," exclaimed the Fisherman. "The main difference between the two is focus. A laser is focused energy. So, start focusing on one task at a time so you can truly give it the attention it deserves. Also, stop focusing on or worrying about what other people are doing because you can't control that. Every time you focus on other people, you are giving away your energy which you will learn more about when you meet the 6th Master Samurai. Instead, focus all your energy on yourself. Your biggest opponent is not the person standing across from you in battle, in school or at your place of work. Your biggest opponent is yourself, so think about what is truly important in your life and be laser-focused on your own dreams and goals and put all your energy and focus into achieving those dreams. Once you can do that, your potential is endless."

3. Remember to Look at The Azaleas

"Don't get me wrong," said the Fisherman with a grin. "As much as you need to do your best and focus on all your tasks and obligations in life, you also have to make time to relax and provide yourself with a reward for your hard work. When it's time to relax, you must focus on relaxing and not think of work and all the obligations and tasks you have yet to complete. What do you like to do to relax?"

Toshi thought about this. "I like to spend time walking around my garden looking at the azaleas, stepping stones, boxwoods and the smooth multi trunk of the crepe myrtle tree."

The Fisherman continued, "That's a great way to relax and unwind. Again, it is important to relax and when it's time to relax, you must also do that to the best of your ability. It's equally important to make time to reward yourself for your hard work. The reward you provide yourself acts to reinforce the habit of working hard in every single task you do."

"I will make sure I always make time for relaxation after a hard day's work," said Toshi.

4. Kaizen

"Small, daily, seemingly insignificant improvements when done consistently over time, do yield staggering results."
–Robin Sharma, The 5 AM Club

The Fisherman continued with his lesson. "To release the blockage in your 3rd energy center to become the highest version of yourself and reach your highest potential, it is important to constantly try to improve yourself. Kaizen is a Japanese term that means continuous improvement in all aspects of your life. Don't settle if you feel like you are meant for more in life. Continue asking questions, continue learning, continue improving, continue making better habits and continue growing. Challenge yourself and tell yourself that you can do what is hard."

"We choose to do things not because they are easy but because they are hard."
–John F. Kennedy

The Fisherman added, "Have the courage to try things that may appear difficult. Courage isn't always the loud roar. Sometimes courage is the quiet voice at the end of the day saying that you will try again tomorrow."

Toshi responded, "I will no longer be afraid of failure. I will challenge myself to do hard things and to constantly improve."

"You are learning," said the Fisherman. "Every day when you try to improve on an aspect in your life, whether it be work-related or health-related, take small steps."

"Can you give me an example," asked Toshi.

"Have you ever been really excited to add a new routine to your day, but no matter how hard you try, you can't motivate yourself to begin that new routine?" asked the Fisherman.

Toshi nodded. "I am constantly telling myself that I am going to begin a routine of exercising for 1 hour every day, but for some reason, when the time comes to exercise, I always have an excuse not to begin."

The Fisherman smiled and said, "If you have a goal to train or exercise more, you should not all of a sudden have a goal of exercising for an hour. When you try to suddenly add an hour of exercise to your routine, the thought of that hour will discourage you from actually beginning that new routine. Instead, you should give yourself a smaller and easier goal to achieve. Instead of having a goal to add 1 hour of exercise to your daily routine, your goal should be to add 5 minutes of exercise. The 5 minutes of exercise is already a great improvement, and since that goal is easier to achieve, it will be easier to add that to your daily routine. When you are able to achieve your goal of exercising for 5 minutes a day, the positive energy it creates in your mind and body for achieving your goal will allow you to make a new goal of increasing the time to exercising 15 minutes a day. You continue this process and add the amount of time you exercise a day in small increments until finally your goal of exercising for 1 hour is achieved."

Toshi thought about this. "This is such a great way of adding new healthy routines in my life. I can see now how small improvements, when done consistently on a daily basis, can lead to great positive changes and results."

"This method of making small improvements in small increments to gain the momentum to make big changes applies to all aspects of your life, not just exercise," said the Fisherman. "If you are trying to wake up earlier, the idea is the same. Instead of trying to wake up 2 hours earlier than your usual time, you should have the goal of waking up 30 minutes earlier. Once you achieve that goal, you can add the amount of time in small increments until your final goal is achieved. If you make small daily improvements, you will not fail to achieve your goals."

Toshi thought about what the Fisherman was teaching and said, "I have always been afraid to fail. The thought of failure brought anxiety to me because I never wanted to let my parents down."

The Fisherman had a look of understanding on his face. "If you try your best and you fail, that is ok. Failure is inevitable and will always lead to growth. The greater the obstacle, the more glory in overcoming it and our greatest glory is not in ever failing but rising every time we fall." The Fisherman then quoted an ancient Japanese proverb,

"Fall down seven times, Stand up eight."

The Fisherman paused, then continued. "There are some people who are so afraid of failing that they don't even want to try. These people have failed before they even began. The people who become the most successful in life are not the ones who are the smartest. It's those that are most resilient. It's the ones who never give up and always try their best that become the most successful in every aspect of their lives."

Toshi added with a large grin, "Even though you are trying to improve, you still have to take time to be present and be grateful, right?"

"Exactly," replied the Fisherman.

"I thought I wouldn't have too many blockages in this energy center because I was confident in my work ethic, but I see there is a lot I still need to work on," said Toshi. "Do you have any guidance on how to respond to obstacles in your life?"

The Fisherman nodded as if to acknowledge that it was a good question. "Once again, you can't control what obstacles you will face in life, but you can control how you respond to them. Instead of focusing on the negativity of a current situation, focus on what you can learn. When faced with an obstacle, ask yourself, 'How can I learn from this? How can I grow from this?'"

The Fisherman continued, "It's important to surrender to what you can't control and take action to what you can control. Whether you complete a task now or later is completely in your control, so don't procrastinate."

"Telling yourself that you will do something someday in the future has killed more dreams than failing ever did."
–Alexandria Maria

The Fisherman added, "Twenty years from now, you will be more disappointed by the things you didn't do than by the ones you did."

No Regrets

Finally, the fisherman added, "When you don't do your best, this leads to regret. The feeling of regret is one of the worst feelings in the world because you will always wonder if you would have succeeded if you had tried harder. Or even worse, you know that you would have succeeded if you tried but were too afraid or lazy to do so. When you have pride in yourself and everything you do, whether at work or in your relationships, whatever the outcome, you will have no regrets because you know you gave it your all and did your best. When you live your life doing your best in everything you do, don't take shortcuts, keep improving and focus on what you can control at this moment, you can live a life with no regrets and release blockages of your 3rd energy source, which is a step closer to living your life to your fullest potential."

Toshi thought about this. He had always felt regret and blamed himself for his sister's death. He knew now that it wasn't his fault. He was 18 years old at the time and only had experience in friendly battles facing an adult man who spent half his life killing women and children. He could not blame himself for the actions of someone else. Toshi knew there was nothing else he could have done that day. He had no regrets.

At that moment, the Fisherman pulled up his line to reveal that he had caught a large and tasty Rainbow Trout.

CHAPTER 6
The Worthy Warrior

"The special thing you have been looking for to complete you, your whole life, is you"

–Course in Miracles

Toshi was told to meet the 4th Samurai Master at the shrine of Gozuryu on the coast at Enoshima island. There is a folktale about a beautiful maiden who descended from the skies and Enoshima island arising from the depths of the water below. An evil dragon named Gozuryu fell in love with the maiden, renounced his evil deeds, and vowed to protect the island from that moment on. People believe that the dragon Gozuryu continues to protect the island to this day, and if you look closely at the hills in Enoshima, you can make out the dragon's shape. Toshi arrived at the shrine of Gozuryu just in time to see the sunset over Mt. Fuji in the distance.

Toshi walked back and forth, looking all around, but could not find the Master. He walked past an elder lady hunched over, wearing clothes full of holes by the shore, trying to pull in a net full of fish. After passing the lady for the 4th time, Toshi heard her say, "My back is in pain. Can you help me bring this basket full of fish to my home? It is not very far away."

Although Toshi was in a rush, he knew meeting the Master could wait. Toshi responded, "Of course, I can help."

The basket of fish was much heavier than Toshi had expected, but they finally made it to an old hut by the water's edge.

"I can take it from here," she said as she thanked him and went inside her home to put the fish away. Moments later, the door opened, and the lady stood in full Samurai armor.

Toshi was surprised to see that the lady was an Onna-Buggeisha, a female Samurai Warrior. Onna-Buggeisha fought alongside Samurai equally to defend their homes, families and honor.

"How come you didn't tell me you were a Master Samurai Warrior?" asked Toshi, feeling his face warm with embarrassment.

"You never asked," responded the Warrior. "Thank you so much for helping me bring the fish home. I'm guessing you are here to learn how to release blockages in your 4th energy center?"

"Yes," said Toshi with a quick bow, his face still red hot.

"The 4th step to reaching your fullest potential and finding peace and lasting fulfillment is to clear the blockage in your 4th energy center, which is located in your heart. To do this, you must learn to love and respect others and, more importantly, love and respect yourself. When you release your 4th energy center, you can achieve your highest potential in your emotional health."

Unconditional Self-worth

> *"Unconditional self-worth is the antidote to low self-worth."*
>
> **–Adia Gooden,** clinical Psychologist

The Warrior said, "When you are born, as you learned before, all 7 of your energy centers are open. You are full of love, and you are absolutely complete as a human being and fully connected with God, as you will learn when you meet the Final Samurai Master. However, from the moment you are born, you are taught by the outside world how you should act, how you should behave and how you should think and feel. As a child, we are taught by teachers that our worth is based on the grades we get in school. Our parents tell us the jobs we need to have to be respected and considered successful. We learn throughout our life to tie our self-worth to what accomplishments we achieve or what materials and wealth we obtain."

"When we don't live up to the unreasonable expectations of the outside world, we are made to feel unworthy and empty inside. Some of us try to fill that emptiness by being busy or by being a perfectionist. We constantly distract ourselves, so we don't have to think about or feel the emptiness inside. Others try to fill that emptiness with unhealthy and unfulfilling relationships. The problem with trying to fill that emptiness with something external is that once that relationship fails or once you are no longer busy and alone, that emptiness is still there."

Toshi thought about this and said, "Before I met my wife and had kids, I always felt an emptiness that I couldn't explain. Indeed, I was always looking to fill that emptiness with unfulfilling relationships and outside distractions."

"Did any of those make you feel less empty inside?" asked the Warrior.

"No, it had the opposite effect. It lowered my feelings of self-worth," responded Toshi.

The Warrior smiled and nodded at Toshi acknowledging his feelings. "Feelings of low self-worth are one of the main causes of mental illness. It can lead to feelings of depression and feelings of anxiety, which can lead to unhealthy addictions such as drugs or alcohol to try to cope with those feelings." The Warrior looked into Toshi's eyes and said, "Unconditional self-worth is the antidote to feeling empty inside."

The Warrior continued, "When you have unconditional self-worth, that knowledge that you are worthy is not reliant on any uncontrollable external factors. When you have unconditional self-worth, it doesn't matter if your relationship fails or if you fail to reach a certain goal. When you know your self-worth, and it is not tied to any external factors, that self-worth will persist even when you face obstacles in life and when life doesn't go as you plan."

"So how do we cultivate the feeling of unconditional self-worth whenever since we were children we were made to feel unworthy?" asked Toshi.

Cultivating Unconditional Self-worth

The Warrior replied, "Cultivating unconditional self-worth is an ongoing practice, and the way you can cultivate unconditional self-worth is to 1) Know that you are complete, 2) Be gentle with yourself and 3) Know you are worthy of respect."

1. You Are Complete

"The sculpture is already complete within the marble block before I start my work. It is already there. I just have to chisel away the superfluous material."
–The Artist, Michelangelo

The Warrior resumed, "When you don't conform to the box society tries to put you in, you are made to feel unworthy, which causes blockages in your heart, your 4th energy center. Once you can release all the blockages in your 7 energy centers, just like you are chiseling away all the superfluous material from you, you will remember and realize that you are already fully complete inside and full of love."

The Warrior continued, "Happiness, Success, Love, Fulfillment and Success in all aspects of your life are your birthright and your destiny. No matter what negative experiences you have had in your life, whatever negative limiting beliefs you have of yourself, or what mistakes you have made, or others have made against you, it's time to forgive yourself and forgive others. Acknowledge and accept everything that has happened in your life. Stop blaming yourself for your mistakes and stop blaming others for their mistakes. Acknowledge and accept the pain you felt and may have caused others. When you acknowledge and accept everything that has happened in your life, you can finally release those negative thoughts and feelings and move forward. You must know that you are innocent, worthy of love and abundance, deserving only of good, and yes, you are complete!"

Toshi felt a warmth surrounding him when he looked into the Warrior's eyes. Her smile made him feel calm and at peace.

The Warrior resumed, "You don't need anyone's affection or approval to be good enough or worthy of love. When someone rejects or abandons you, it isn't actually about you. There is nothing wrong with you. It's about them and their insecurities and limitations. It's time to accept yourself the way you are. Let go of the expectations people have of you and let go of the expectations you have of the people around you. Let go of how you think society expects you to look or feel. Instead, focus on being and accepting yourself for who you are. Your worth is not contingent on other people's acceptance of you. Your worth is inherent. You exist, and therefore you matter. You are allowed to voice your thoughts and feelings."

Toshi thought to himself and realized that all the stress and pressure he had felt were from the perfectionist expectations others had placed on him and the unrealistic expectations he had placed on himself. All his life, all he wanted was to make his parents and his sister proud. He felt he didn't deserve love from his parents and others in his life because he was unable to save his sister. Toshi knew it was time to let those feelings go and to forgive himself because he was worthy of love and forgiveness.

2. Be Gentle with Yourself

"Have you ever loved someone so deeply that you would do anything for them? Make that person yourself!"

The Warrior continued, "Before you can love anybody else in your life, you have to first learn to love yourself. Remember to take time for yourself to recharge, reflect and think about your life experiences and what you want for your future. You need to make time for yourself for self-care. To release the blockage in your heart, you must remind yourself that you are worthy of love, happiness, respect and abundance in all aspects of your life."

Toshi thought about taking more time for self-care and said, "I feel guilty when I take time for my self-care. I feel that I should be strong, and instead of taking time taking care of myself, I should spend more time taking care of my family."

"Self-Care is Not Selfish, It's Sacred," said the Warrior with a warm smile while placing her hand on Toshi's shoulder. "You must fall in love with taking care of yourself and fall in love with healing so that you can become the best version of yourself. When you become the best version of yourself, you are also improving the lives of

everyone around you. So, taking care of yourself is also taking care of your family and the people you love."

This made sense to Toshi. Toshi wanted to become the highest version of himself, so he could live life to the fullest and be at his best for himself and his family.

The Warrior continued with her lesson. "It's ok and normal to want external validation. We all need support, love and attention from others. Wanting that isn't wrong. The problem arises when external validation is your only source, and you rely on it entirely. You must learn to love yourself unconditionally and not rely on something external for you to feel loved, worthy or reassured of your self-worth. It's time to take back your power because you are worthy of love."

"If you fully love yourself, the fear you have inside will slowly disappear. If you can accept yourself for who you are, you will no longer have to fear what others think about you. You no longer need any outside source of affirmation of love because you have it within you."

The Warrior looked at Toshi patiently, "You are worthy of happiness, and nobody has the power to take away your happiness unless you give that power to them. Remove from your mind that something must occur in your life first before you can be happy. Most people think that they can be happy once they make a certain amount of money, have a certain career, achieve certain results, or get married. As you have learned from releasing your 3rd energy center, you cannot control outcomes. Since you cannot control certain outcomes, you must do your best to enjoy the here and now and be happy in the journey. You deserve happiness now. The positive energy from the happiness you feel will bring more positivity in your life and increase the chances that you will obtain the outcome you so desire."

Toshi gave the Warrior an intriguing look and said, "Sometimes when I am too happy, I get worried because I feel that since life is always balanced, something negative will come into my life."

The Warrior said, chuckling, "It's funny that so many people feel that way. No negativity will come into your life if you are too happy. When you are happy, you can manifest more happiness to come into your life if you follow the lessons of the 6th Master Samurai you will meet soon. The truth is happiness is your nature and your destiny."

3. You Are Worthy of Respect

The Warrior continued, "You are also worthy of respect. Being in our lives is a privilege that needs to be earned. That privilege is revoked when you are treated poorly, disrespected or hurt. It is important to have self-respect and self-worth, so surround yourself with people who respect you and your self-worth. Having the courage to say no to the little things in life will give you the power to say yes to the big things. You must do everything you can to protect your time, energy, body spirit and space."

"The misconception by many is that the best way to earn respect is by instilling fear in others. There are many leaders and bosses that try to gain respect by making others fear them. The respect you gain by instilling fear is not true respect. The secret to gaining respect from others is by showing them respect. While you are worthy of respect, it is equally important to be respectful to others. See the greatness in everyone around you and know that you are not better or superior to anyone else. No matter who you are interacting with, understand that each individual has their personal history, experiences and personal trauma. Regardless of how much money they make or how successful they are in life or what obstacles they may be currently facing, they are a spiritual being connected with all of us. They are also worthy of love, happiness and abundance."

Toshi knew that cultivating unconditional self-worth was something he needed to work on. For all these years, he blamed himself for his sister's death. He never felt he was worthy of love or forgiveness, so he tried to fill that emptiness with meaningless battles and live up to unreasonable expectations others had placed on him and those he had placed on himself. Toshi now understood that no matter what mistakes he made in the past, he was complete and worthy of love and forgiveness. At that moment, Toshi finally forgave himself for his sister's death. Toshi felt an emotion he had not felt in years. Pure happiness.

CHAPTER 7
The Purposeful Priest

Everyone has a unique gift; your job is to find out what that gift is and share it with the world.

The 5th Master Samurai was at Kiyomizu Dera, the Temple of the Pure Water Spring. This is one of the most famous Buddhist temples in Kyoto, Japan. The temple is known for its wooden stage extending from its main hall, over 40 feet above the hillside below. The main hall and the stage were built without nails and houses the temple's object of worship, a small statue of the eleven-faced, thousand-armed female goddess of mercy. At the base of the main hall is a waterfall divided into 3 streams. Each stream is rumored to have a different benefit, longevity, success and fortune in one's love life. However, drinking from all three streams is considered greedy.

Toshi arrived at the wooden stage of Kiyomizu Dera and met with a Priest wearing a traditional robe. From the wooden stage, Toshi could see the top of numerous cherry and maple trees that have erupted into a sea of deep reds, maroon, oranges, greens and yellows.

The Priest immediately introduced himself, "I am the 5th Samurai Master. Are you here to learn how to release the blockage of your 5th energy center located in your throat?"

"Yes," replied Toshi. "It is an honor to meet you."

"The honor is mine," said the Priest with a deep bow.

Live A Purposeful Life

"He who has a why to live can bear almost any how."

–Friedrich Nietzche

The Priest leaned toward Toshi and gestured with his hands as he spoke. "To find lasting peace and fulfillment in your life, you must live a life of purpose. When you live a life of purpose, you can overcome any obstacles that you may face. Most people, however, seek purpose in all the wrong places. When they look for purpose, they are searching from a mindset that was given to them by their parents or society. They mistakenly believe their purpose in life is to gain material wealth, achieve a certain position in society or obtain some other earthly goal. They fail to understand that, contrary to what they have been told, peace and fulfillment are not automatic byproducts of physical wealth and success. From a young age, you are taught by your parents, movies and society at large that if you obtain physical wealth or achieve success, you will find peace, fulfillment and happiness. The truth is it is often the people who have accomplished the most in life who feel empty and unfulfilled. So many people wake up in the morning unhappy about their jobs and dreading their daily responsibilities and commitments. No matter how successful they are or how much physical wealth they have achieved, they feel unfulfilled and empty because they are not living a purposeful life. Instead of doing what they love and are passionate about, they are doing what they believe they should be doing and what they feel is expected of them. There is a time in everyone's life where you have to stop and ask yourself, 1) Are you where you want to be at the moment? 2) Are you doing what you feel you are meant to do at the moment? and 3) Are you living a purposeful life?"

"I have become one of the most famous Samurai in Japan and achieved what most can only dream of. Yet, I feel unfulfilled and empty inside. I know that success and fame did not bring me the peace and fulfillment I desired," said Toshi. "What are the steps to live a purposeful life?"

The Priest responded, "To live a purposeful life that brings peace and lasting fulfillment, you must 1) Discover your unique gift, 2) Share that unique gift with the world, and 3) Constantly Give and Grow."

1. Discover Your Unique Gift

"Excellence only comes when you do something that truly resonates with your soul."

–Gaur Gopal Das

The Priest continued, "The first step to living a purposeful life is to discover your unique gift. You do not have to compete to prove yourself. Everyone has a unique gift inside of them that no one else has. These could be talents, interests you are passionate about or special skills that you don't even know you have yet."

Toshi said softly, "I don't think I have ever asked myself what I am passionate about. Since I was a child, the only motivation for my actions was to make my sister and parents proud. My father expected me to be a great Samurai, so I did everything possible to meet that expectation. When I think about it now, after all the battles I have been in, fighting and killing another human being has never made me happy. I guess I don't know what my purpose or passion is. I have always gone through the motions down the path others had set for me. Master, how can I find my purpose and find out what I am passionate about?"

The Priest looked directly at Toshi and said compassionately, "To discover what you are passionate about, you must do what you love and love what you do. What do you love to do? Stop doing what hurts you and start doing what heals you. Stop doing what gives you anxiety and start doing what brings you peace. Stop doing what brings you fear and start doing what brings you love. Stop doing what brings you unhappiness and start doing what brings you happiness. Instead of doing what society tells you to do or what people in your life expect you to do, do what you love and do what brings you peace and happiness. That is the way to discover what you are passionate about."

"Is it that easy?" asked Toshi.

"It truly is," replied the Priest. "Sometimes, to discover your true passions, it could help to think about your childhood ambitions and dreams. What did you enjoy doing as a child? What brought you happiness as a child? What adult occupation did you dream of having as a child? You get various answers when you ask a child what they want to be when they grow up. Some children will tell you they want to be the Shogun, the President, a professional athlete, an artist or an inventor of time travel. Children do not place restrictions on themselves as adults do. Children dare to dream big, and no dream is too impossible for them to achieve. The problem is that as they age, society starts limiting them. For example, teachers tell them that their dreams are impossible or parents may tell them that their dream job will not pay the bills. When children are taught that their dreams are not realistic, their expectations of themselves and their confidence in their ideas both decline.

Their creativity gets suppressed as they begin doing what is safe by trying to be like everyone around them."

"Now that I think about it, you are right," said Toshi while he walked towards the edge of the wooden stage, looking out over the top of the trees below. "When my son was younger, he loved to follow me around the garden and always told me he wanted to be a gardener. I told him he needed to be a respected Samurai like his father and grandfather. As he got older, he stopped talking about gardening. I never realized it until now, but I was already suppressing my son's creativity and passions even at such a young age."

"Unfortunately, it's a cycle that repeats itself because when our children grow up, they will pass on to their children what they learned from us," said the Priest. Oftentimes our goals and dreams as a child are what we are truly passionate about which we have been suppressing due to the restrictions and expectations placed on us by society. Remembering what brought us joy and happiness as a child can help us find our passions in life and once you discover your passions, you must pursue them."

The Priest continued, "Sometimes to find your unique gift that you can share with the world, you must realize that you are in the strongest position to serve and help the type of person you once were. It's important to think about what challenges and obstacles you have overcome in life because nobody has gone through the exact same struggles as you. You can then use your experiences to help others in a similar situation."

"Once we discover what our unique gift is, should we drop everything in our life to pursue our passions?" asked Toshi.

The Priest responded, "Understandably, you may be in a situation where you have a job or responsibility that you are not passionate about but brings you security. I am not saying you need to leave that job. It's ok to stay at a job that brings you security, but you must find things you are truly passionate about on the side that bring you fulfillment. Who knows, maybe the thing you are passionate about will lead to success and security and that may turn into your full time job or responsibility. We spend so much time working every day. The key is to find time for things that bring you love, happiness and peace because those are the things that could lead to unlocking your true purpose in life. Following your purpose in life and sharing it with the world will lead you to your supreme destiny. Doing what you love and loving what you do is the first step to living a purposeful life that will bring you lasting peace and fulfillment and release the blockages of your 5th energy center in your throat."

"When I really think about it, what really brought me joy as a child was not the physical contact or fighting aspect of martial arts. What brought me the most joy was learning and teaching. It brought me so much happiness when my sister and I would learn and teach each other new techniques," said Toshi.

The Priest smiled. "Perhaps, your unique gift is not fighting, but teaching. Just like your father."

Toshi loved the thought of this. He was much more similar to his father than he had ever imagined.

2. Share Your Gift with The World

The Priest continued, "The second step to living a purposeful life is to share your unique gift with the world. When you find out what you are passionate about and what your unique gift is, you must share that gift with the world. Vincent Van Gogh couldn't sell his artwork when he was alive. Even though he wasn't able to sell his paintings, he continued to paint. Now, his artwork is recognized as one of the deepest expressions of art and shared all over the world. Sharing your gift with the world doesn't always mean sharing it with thousands or even hundreds of people. Sometimes, it's enough to share your gift and use your experiences to have a positive impact on one other individual."

Toshi asked, "How can sharing my gift with one other individual help anyone."

The Priest responded, "We all have the ability to have a positive impact on other people's lives. For example, imagine a person who loves to sing. She might be walking down a path, and another person who is having a terrible day may hear her beautiful voice and feel better. There is no gift that is insignificant. Your gift may be that you have a positive and loving energy about you, and the way you share that gift with the world is through your smile. Positive changes in life always start small. Changing the world to make it a better place begins one person at a time."

3. Giving and Growing

"The secret to life is giving and growing."

–Tony Robbins

"The third step to living a purposeful life that brings peace and lasting fulfillment is constantly giving to others and constantly growing. Most people are focused on themselves, their desires and their wants. The most consistent way you can feel happy and fulfilled in life is to focus on something or someone that you want to give to that is greater than yourself. This could be God, your family or people less fortunate than you."

Toshi was interested in the Priest's lesson. "So, giving to others will make me feel happier and fulfilled?"

"Yes, of course," responded the Priest. "Giving to others activates a region in your brain that makes you feel pleasure and contentment. It can lower your stress levels, lower your blood pressure and increase your mood."

"I never knew giving to others had so many benefits," replied Toshi.

The Priest nodded. "The more you give, the better you feel. You don't have to give anything material like money. If you give to God, it could be a small prayer or a conscious decision that you will do your best in everything you do during the day as a dedication to God. If you give to your family, you can give them your love, your time or most importantly, your full attention. If you are giving to a stranger, it could be a smile, a compliment or even a simple silent prayer wishing them well."

"Who knew it would be so easy to find happiness and fulfillment through giving," said Toshi.

"When you give, though, it can't be from a place where you are giving just because you are expecting something in return," said the Priest. When you give, it must be from a place in your heart where you are happy to help others. It must be from a place of love. You will learn more about the energies, frequencies and vibrations of giving when you meet the 6th Master Samurai."

The Priest added, "To live a purposeful life, you must also constantly grow. The secret to fulfillment and happiness is progress and achieving goals. It's not really about achieving the goals but more about who you become in pursuing those goals. You feel most fulfilled when your life matches the plans and expectations you have for your own life. When you feel like your life is not going according to your plans or that your life is not where you have expected it to be, that brings unfulfillment. When your life is not progressing according to your plans or expectations, you must make changes and improve your life so that your life can match your plan or expectation. If you cannot make improvements to your life so that your life can match your plan or expectation, then you have to change your plans and expectations. That is how you continually grow and progress by creating and achieving new goals you have set for yourself."

Toshi looked like he was in deep thought. He thought about the hundreds of battles he had been in and the pressure he put on himself to be the best. He thought each victory would bring him happiness and fulfillment, but each victory made him feel emptier and lonelier than before. After hearing what the Priest said, Toshi realized that he was never growing or progressing. Being a Samurai in Japan who never lost a battle was an unrealistic expectation that brought on too much stress and pressure, especially since he had yet to fight the hooded Samurai.

At that moment, Toshi let go of all the unrealistic expectations he had placed on himself. Instead of being the Samurai who never lost a battle, he decided to be the Samurai who always did his best and had no regrets. He would follow his passion for teaching and share his gift with the world. Those expectations were more realistic and would allow him to grow and achieve his goals.

Toshi had begun to release the blockages in his 5th energy center.

The 6th Samurai Master was at Fushimi Inari Shrine in Kyoto. The shrine was famous for its thousands of red gates, which straddle a number of stairs that lead up into the wooded forest of the sacred Mount Inari.

Toshi traveled to the sacred Mount Inari and walked up an endless flight of stairs passing thousands of red gates. When Toshi reached the top of the mountain, he couldn't believe who was standing at the top waiting for him.

CHAPTER 8

The Shogun and The Power of His Mind

"Where Your Mind Goes, Energy Flows. Where Energy Flows, The Universe Shows."

The Shogun of Japan at the time was a direct descendant of one of the greatest Samurai in history, Tokugawa Ieyasu. The Sengoku Period in Japan, known as the Warring States Period, was a turbulent and violent time in Japanese history of near-constant civil war. Various Samurai warlords and clans fought for power over Japan. Tokugawa Ieyasu was credited for unifying Japan when he became the first Shogun of the Tokugawa Shogunate, which presided over 250 years of peace and prosperity in the country.

Standing in front of Toshi was none other than the Shogun himself.

Toshi immediately bowed his head as a show of respect. "Shogun, it is such a great honor to be in your presence."

The Shogun replied, "I have been waiting to meet you for many years. Your father was a legendary warrior in his days. I had offered him a position in my royal guard numerous times as my personal bodyguard and riches beyond his wildest dreams. Only the best fighters in Japan are offered that position. He respectfully declined every time and said teaching his son and daughter and spending time with his family was his purpose and worth more to him than any amount of riches. You and I know that finding your purpose and following your passions releases blockages in your 5th energy center, so I respected his decision. Regretfully I was never able to meet your sister, but the honor is mine to meet you here today finally. I will teach you everything I can about how my ancestors used the power of their thoughts to manifest anything they wanted in their reality."

Your Thoughts Manifest Your Reality

The Shogun took a deep breath and began his lesson. "Let me tell you the story of a well-known Kabuki actor. He was not always as famous as he is now. At the beginning of his career, he went on numerous auditions and was rejected for the role each time. He began having doubts about his career but knew the power of his thoughts and his mind. He wrote 3 words on a piece of washi paper that read "50 gold coins", dated it ten years into the future and tucked it into his kimono. Throughout the years, no matter how many auditions he was unsuccessful at, he would take out the washi paper and visualize that he was getting paid 50 gold coins. Ten years later, he was in a Kabuki play that jump-started his career and guess how much he was paid for his role?"

Toshi couldn't believe it. "50 gold coins?"

"That's right," said the Shogun with a smile. "The power of the mind is more powerful than you can ever imagine. Your thoughts manifest your reality."

"I'm not sure what the term manifest means," said Toshi, slightly embarrassed.

The Shogun looked at Toshi patiently and said, "It means when you create something in your reality through the power of your thoughts, mind and actions."

"This is so interesting. I never knew your thoughts could create your reality," said Toshi.

"It's incredible once you know how powerful your mind is. Let me give you another example. Every time a new medicine comes out, it must be tested on sick patients to see how effective it is. One of the ways of testing is by giving some of the sick patients the actual medicine while the other patients are given a placebo. The placebo looks like the medicine they are testing, but it is made of an inactive substance, such as sugar. The participants in the test do not know if they are receiving the actual medicine or the placebo. Studies have shown that the sick patients receiving the placebo still get better because their mind thinks it is getting real medicine and tells its body that it needs to heal. In essence, their thoughts are creating their reality."

"This is so amazing," exclaimed Toshi. "How does our mind create reality? How does it work?"

Energy, Frequency and Vibrations

"If you want to find the secrets to the Universe, think in terms of energy, frequency and vibration."
-Nicola Tesla

The Shogun replied, "The secret to manifesting all your dreams, desires and goals is understanding energy, frequency and vibration."

"I've heard people talk about energy, frequency and vibration before, but I never knew what they meant," said Toshi.

"Let me explain," said the Shogun. "Every thought and emotion have a certain energy, vibration and frequency. Some emotions such as peace, joy and love have a higher energy, while feelings such shame, guilt, fear and desire have lower energy. Every energy, vibration and frequency you emit attracts similar energies, vibrations and frequencies to you."

"Can you give me an example of this," asked Toshi.

"Yes," replied the Shogun. "Think of a television. When you turn on the television and change the channel, the energy, electricity and frequency flow into and through the television, allowing you to see what you want. When you want to see something different, you change the energy and frequency flowing into and through the television by changing the channel. Think of your mind as the television constantly emitting and receiving energy, frequencies and vibrations. When there is something in your life you don't want to see, you have to change the energy, frequency and vibration in your mind so that you can receive and see what you want in your life."

"You have explained it in a way that allows me to understand it more clearly," said Toshi, focused on what the Shogun was teaching. "What are the specific steps I need to take to manifest my dreams and goals into reality?"

The Secret to Manifesting Your Reality

"You don't manifest what you want. You manifest what you are."

The Shogun explained, "There are 3 steps to take to manifest all your desires, dreams and goals into reality. You must 1) Become what you want to manifest, 2) Take action and 3) Surrender."

"These sound pretty simple to me. I wonder why more people aren't using the power of manifestation in their lives?" asked Toshi.

The Shogun replied, "These seem like simple steps, but they require a lot of focus and trust. A lot of people are good at one or two of the steps but need more work on the other. Once you can master all 3 steps, you can manifest anything you want into your reality."

Become What You Want to Manifest

The Shogun continued, "The first step is you must become what you want to manifest."

"How can someone become what they want to manifest?" asked Toshi.

The Shogun explained, "To become what you want to manifest, you must believe that what you want is already yours. You must emit the frequency that you have already received and achieved your specific desire, dream or goal."

Toshi looked confused. "How do you emit the frequency that you have already achieved those goals?"

The Shogun went on, "You must first be extremely clear on your dreams, desires and goals. Most people want to be successful in life but aren't clear and specific about what success means to them. Do they want financial success, do they want happiness, do they want a successful relationship or all the above? You have to contemplate long and hard and be extremely focused and clear on what you specifically want and desire."

Toshi thought about this and said, "I can use the quiet times while meditating to have clarity in my mind on what my specific goals in life are."

The Shogun nodded and said, "That is the perfect time to focus on what you want in life. Once you are focused and clear on your specific desires, dreams and goals, you need to imagine how you would feel when you achieve those goals and hold onto those feelings. It's important that if you want to attract happiness in your life, you have to emit the energy, frequency and vibration of happiness by feeling and thinking about happiness. If you want success in your life, you must emit the energy, frequency and vibration of success by feeling and thinking about success. Let me give you an example. Before you go into a battle, what do you think about?"

Toshi thought about all the battles he had been in. "Every time I go into battle, I only think about winning the battle. I can already visualize in my mind all the techniques I will use to be victorious, and I picture in my mind me standing over my defeated opponent. I imagine how I will feel when I win the fight."

The Shogun had a big smile on his face. "That is so wonderful. You had already been using the power of your mind to manifest victories for all these years without you even knowing it. Let me ask you another question, before you go into battle, do you ever say to yourself, "I hope I win this battle?"'

Toshi again thought about all the battles he had been in. "I never use the word hope. I was confident I would win in every battle I have been in because I prepared so much for them."

The Shogun smiled again. "That brings me to a very important point. When you tell yourself that you want something or hope for something, your mind hears that you have doubt and are lacking the thing you actually want. When the energy, frequency and vibration of lack or scarcity enter your mind, it attracts more scarcity into your life. That's why instead of focusing on how you "want" to win a particular battle, you succeeded because you always imagined and visualized in your head you had already won the battle."

Toshi laughed and said, "I guess I always have been manifesting my victories."

Both men laughed. The Shogun added, "The secret most successful people have, including my ancestors and yourself, is that we all have an unwavering belief and confidence in ourselves and what we can accomplish. Once we set our minds on something, we remove all doubt from our minds. That is important when you manifest your dreams and goals into reality."

The Shogun went on, "When you tell yourself, I really want this job or I hope I don't fail this job interview, what your mind hears is that you doubt that you will get the job you want. The energy, frequency and vibration of the doubt in your mind will create more scarcity in your life. Instead, you must tell yourself that the job is already yours and visualize how you will feel when you get that job. When the feeling of success and the accomplishment of your dreams and goals enters your mind, it attracts more of those energies into your life."

The Shogun continued, "I'll give you another example. In a relationship, you shouldn't look for the perfect person. Once again, if you are looking, then that tells your mind that there is something you are lacking in life. Instead, you should become the person your dream partner would want. When you become that perfect partner yourself, it attracts the perfect partner into your life."

"I understand now that I need to become what I want to manifest," said Toshi.

1. The Importance of Your Word

The Shogun paused for a moment and added, "Not only are your thoughts important. The things you say out loud are very important as well. Similar to your thoughts, you must focus on what you say. Many say things like, "I don't think I will get the job" or "I hope I can become successful." Once again, this tells your mind that you have lack and scarcity in some aspect of your life which will manifest more of the same. Instead, you have to always be consciously focused on what you are saying not only to yourself in your mind but out loud to others as well. You must be confident and positive every time you open your mouth. You must remember how powerful you are and how powerful your mind and words are."

"That is something I need to work on," admitted Toshi. "Sometimes, when people compliment my fighting skills, I don't want to appear too arrogant, so I will say, "I'm not that good of a fighter" or "It was mostly luck."

The Shogun leaned into Toshi and said, "Arrogance is never a good thing. However, it is acceptable to be humble and confident at the same time, especially if you have worked hard to get to where you are. Instead of diminishing all your hard work and skills, why not just say thank you or tell them that you worked hard to get to where you are, and you appreciate their compliment."

Toshi agreed. "I should be more focused on the things I say."

The Shogun replied, "One suggestion I want to make to you is to replace the word "should" with "could" in your vocabulary."

Toshi looked confused. "I don't understand what you mean by that."

The Shogun explained, "When you constantly tell yourself you "should" do something, it makes you feel guilt, pressure or even resentment when you don't or cannot complete the particular task or obligation. Guilt, pressure and resentment are low vibrational energies and frequencies which will attract similar low vibrational energies and frequencies to you. When you tell yourself you "could" do something, it instead allows you to be in control and decide whether doing that task or obligation is in your best interest and for your highest good for that moment."

"That makes sense," said Toshi. "There are so many tasks and obligations I tell myself I should complete every day. It leads to me feeling overwhelmed and anxious. It would be nice to be gentler with myself and not give myself too much pressure to complete all those obligations as long as I know I am trying my best. I am learning so much from this lesson. I will no longer say words that diminish myself or my worth. Is there anything else I can do to help me become what I want to manifest?"

2. Vision Boards and Journaling

The Shogun smiled and nodded his head. "One way to make your thoughts even more powerful and become what you want to manifest is to put your thoughts into writing. The art of journaling or keeping a book where you write down your thoughts, intentions, goals and dreams is a very powerful and effective tool because you are reinforcing your thoughts by writing them down, which emits the energy, frequency and vibration of what you desire and therefore opening yourself up to receiving more of the same. However, similarly to your thoughts and your words, you have to be careful of what you write. If you write the words, "I want success, I want love or I want happiness," it tells your mind you are lacking those things in your life. When you have the energy of scarcity in your mind, it will attract those similar energies into your life."

"Instead, you should write your goals and dreams as if you have already accomplished them, such as, "I am successful, I am loved, and I am happy and grateful." The positive energies in those words will then attract more success, love and happiness into your life."

"I understand," said Toshi. "I see the value in journaling positive thoughts every day to raise those energies in my mind."

"Have you ever seen a vision board?" asked the Shogun.

"I don't think I have," replied Toshi.

"A vision board is a similar concept where you collect images of the things you want to manifest in your life and place them on a board where you can look at it every day. Again, it's important when you look at these images not to desire them from a mindset of lack but to think of them as if you have already accomplished and achieved them. The more you see the things you want to manifest in life, the more your mind will be convinced that those things are already in your life and therefore be open to attracting those things."

"That is such a great idea," said Toshi. "I can't wait to try these techniques."

3. Giving to Others

The Shogun continued, "Another way to become what you want to manifest is to constantly give to others. Not just to others but yourself as well."

"This is very interesting!" said Toshi.

"Absolutely," said the Shogun. "When we give, it tells our mind that we are abundant in that which we are giving. When our mind is convinced we are abundant in that which we are giving, it raises the energy in our mind, therefore, attracting more of that energy into our life."

"I'm not sure I understand," said Toshi. "Can you give me an example of how giving will attract more in your life."

"Yes," replied the Shogun. "Some of the wealthiest people in the world are also the biggest givers who are constantly donating their money to charities. When you give money to those who need it, you are telling your mind that you are financially abundant. That creates a specific energy in your mind that attracts more of that same energy of financial abundance into your life. So, the more money you give, the more financial abundance you attract in your life."

"Does this only work for money?" asked Toshi.

"No," said the Shogun. "This applies to everything you want to receive more of in your life. If you give more love, you will attract more love into your life. If you give happiness to others, you will attract more happiness in your life."

"So, if I want more success, I should help others achieve success?" asked Toshi.

"Exactly," said the Shogun. "The important thing is that when you give, it has to be from a place in your heart where you are happy you are helping others. If you give, but you are thinking about how much money you don't have, or giving just because you want something in return, then that will lead to negative energies in your mind, which will attract more negativity and scarcity. So always give from a place of love."

Take Action

"The second step to manifest all your desires, dreams and goals into reality is taking action," continued the Shogun. With a stern look, the Shogun added, "No matter how strong our minds are, you can't expect to achieve your goals with the power of your mind alone. For example, there are so many people who are experts at the first step of believing and becoming what they want to manifest. One person may be unemployed and sitting on his tatami every day thinking about all the financial success he will have in the future. The problem is, if he doesn't take action and go on job interviews, he will never achieve the success he wants. Another person may constantly be thinking about meeting their perfect partner, but if that person never takes action to go on dates or take action to improve themselves physically, mentally, emotionally and spiritually, then they will not meet that perfect partner out there."

The Shogun continued, "After focusing all your mind on your dreams and goals, you still have to take action by doing your best to achieve those dreams and goals and not give up as you learned from the 3rd Samurai Master, the Fisherman."

"Everything's coming together," said Toshi. "I understand how all the energy centers are connected to each other."

"That's right," said the Shogun. "There is a balance between the importance of preparation and being ready to take action. Some people are so hesitant to take action because they feel more preparation is needed. The problem with that is, they may put off taking action indefinitely because the reality is you can never prepare too much."

"So how do you know when you have prepared enough to take action?" asked Toshi.

The Shogun smiled and said, "The final Samurai Master will have the answer to this question."

Surrender

"God answers prayers in 3 ways. 1) Yes, because it will help you become the highest version of yourself, 2) No, because you deserve better and 3) Not yet, because the best is yet to come."

The Shogun continued, "The third and final step to manifest your desires, dreams and goals into reality is often the hardest for people. No matter how strong your mind is, no matter how much action you take, you must still take the 3rd and final step and surrender."

Toshi looked confused. "Surrender? I don't like to surrender. I would never surrender in my life because I will always fight to the end."

The Shogun explained, "This is exactly why this last step is always the most difficult for people to master. We are taught by society that surrendering is negative and a sign of weakness when it takes a lot of strength, courage and faith to surrender. Some people believe in God, while others believe in the Universe, source, energy or your higher self. Regardless of what you believe in, the final step after you manifest your dreams and goals in your mind and take action in achieving those goals is to surrender to something higher than yourself and trust that God, Source, the Universe will bring to you what you are desiring and manifesting. Instead of always trying to control things in our lives that really are beyond our control to get the things we want in life, we must surrender to a higher power and have faith that we will be given the things we truly need in life. That higher power may not bring it to you at the exact moment you want, but you will receive abundance in all aspects of your life at the best moment for you."

Toshi responded, "I can understand how surrendering can be hard for people. I would have a hard time surrendering because I would constantly be thinking about how I'm going to achieve those dreams and goals."

"How it will happen is not your concern or job," replied the Shogun. "Allow the energy of the Universe to take care of that for you. When you are trying to think about how it will happen, you are again emitting a frequency of lack. Don't get caught up in the how, when or where. There may be times when you feel disappointment because you have not achieved a specific goal, dream or desire. During those times, you must not give up. Failure to reach your goals just means that God, Source, the Universe has a better plan for you that you may not even be able to comprehend at the moment."

"This has been a life-changing lesson for me. Thank you for teaching me the secret to manifesting anything I want into my reality," said Toshi with a deep bow.

The Shogun bowed back and said, "Toshi, you are the architect of your own life. Don't ever forget that you have the power to create the masterpiece that is you."

CHAPTER 9

The Final Master

"I am the taste in water, the light in the moon and sun, the sacred syllable Om, the fragrance in the earth, the brilliance in fire, the life in the living...I am the father of the Universe and its mother...I am the beginning and the end...I am the consciousness of all beings"

–Bhagavad Gita, Translation by Stephen Mitchell

Toshi couldn't believe how much he had learned on this journey, and he was excited to meet the final Master Samurai. Toshi was in disbelief when he was told by the Shogun where to find the final Master.

The Shogun said, "You will meet the final Master Samurai in Shakujii Village."

"What?" asked Toshi with his mouth wide open, losing his composure for the first time. "Are you telling me the final Master Samurai lives in the village where I grew up?"

"Yes," replied the Shogun. "There, you will learn the most important lesson about your Supreme Destiny and how to release the blockage of your crown, the area above your head."

Toshi traveled quickly back to his village, eager to meet the final Master Samurai. He wondered who it could be. Could it be one of his neighbors he grew up with? Or perhaps it could be a lady at the market? The first person Toshi went to was his mother. "Mother, do you know where I can find a Master Samurai who lives in our village?"

His mother looked confused. "Master Samurai? I have never heard of a Master Samurai living in our village. Maybe you can go ask our neighbors to see if they have any information."

Toshi rushed out the door and asked everyone he saw, but nobody knew of any Master Samurai who lived in the village. It got dark outside, and the villagers returned to their homes for the night, but Toshi was still no closer to finding the Master Samurai than when he first arrived. As Toshi continued to walk around trying to figure out who the Master Samurai could be, he realized he had ended up at the exact location where his sister was killed. Only this time, he did not feel scared or alone. Maybe releasing the blockages in his first energy center and learning to let go of past trauma had helped him feel stronger and more secure in himself?

Toshi walked down the path lined by stone lanterns on both sides to get to Shakujii Lake. Once he got to the lake, it was dark, but for the light from the stars and moon in the sky that reflected onto the lake surface. Toshi felt so much peace at that moment, looking at the stillness of the water. Toshi kept wondering where and who the final Master Samurai could be. As Toshi gazed into the water, he saw something that made him realize who he was looking for. He saw a reflection of a man who had kindness in his eyes. A man who had been through many obstacles in life was doing his best to improve himself so he could reach his highest potential physically, emotionally, mentally and spiritually. Toshi realized who the final Master Samurai was. The final Master Samurai was himself.

Tat Tvam Asi, "You Are That. That You Are"

"The journey to God is merely the reawakening of the knowledge of where you are always and what you are forever."
–Course in Miracles

To release the blockage of his 7th energy center, the crown above his head, Toshi needed to reach his highest potential in his spiritual health. Underneath the stars and moon, looking at his reflection in the lake, at that very moment, Toshi felt connected to every living thing around him, and he realized that we are all one. Toshi looked at the countless shining stars in the sky and thought about the origin and evolution of the Universe. He thought about the Big Bang Theory, which supported the idea that the Universe began almost 14 billion years ago from one single source. We have all emerged from that one infinite source, so the infinite cosmic forces of creation are within each one of us. Some people refer to that one source of creation as God. Therefore, since we all emerged from God, we are all connected with God and have God within us.

"Quantum theory forces us to see the Universe not as a collection of physical objects, but rather as a complicated web of relations between the various parts of a unified whole."
–Fritjof Capra, The Tao of Physics

Toshi thought about the teachings of Jesus who said in John 17:21, *"That all of them may be one, Father, just as you are in me and I am in you."* Toshi thought about the Bhagavad Gita, which states, *"God dwells in you, as you"* and a classic Arab proverb that says, *"Whoever knows himself, knows his Lord."* Toshi thought about the teachings of Rumi, who said, *"We are one. Everything in the Universe is within "* and the teachings of Buddhism that we all need to look inside because all living beings possess the Buddha nature. Throughout history, there have been teachings that we are all connected to God, the cosmos, to the Universe and to the source of all things.

Toshi looked down into the smooth surface of the lake and saw the reflection of the moon within it. As he looked closer, he saw the faces of his wife, his sons and daughter in the reflection smiling back at him. Tears ran down his face as he felt a sudden surge of love and energy vibrating throughout his body. He saw the 7 of them, including himself, holding hands, forming a circle, shining light and love on each other during times of darkness. The faces of his wife and children were so clear in the reflection, and looking at them brought Toshi love and peace he had never felt before. He heard a voice inside of him telling him that this is what life is all about.

Life is about Love. Love is what is important. Everything else is trivial.

What Matters Most in Life

> *"God is Love. The shift from fear to love is a miracle. Love in your mind produces love in your life. Fear in your mind produces fear in your life. The perfect you isn't something you need to create because God already created it. The perfect you is the love within you."*
>
> **–A Return to Love, Marianne Williamson**

What matters most in life is Love. Because God is love. 2 John 1:6 states, "He has commanded us to love one another." The most important lesson on Earth is learning how to love which is why we have a whole lifetime to learn it. When someone is on their deathbed, they don't want to be surrounded by material objects such as money, trophies or certificates of achievements they've collected in life. Instead, they want to be surrounded by the people they love. They don't think about how they should have worked harder to make more money while they were young and healthy. They think about how they should have spent more time with the people they love.

Love is what life is all about. The greatest legacy you can leave in life is the relationships you made and having a positive impact on everyone you came into contact with, not the physical wealth you accumulated.

Toshi thought about his wife. She would not be the screen he would project his unmet needs and wants. Instead, she was a partner whom he would cherish. Their purpose together was not to complete each other but to celebrate each other since they were both already whole. The relationship would not be used to bring each other down or to try to make the other partner conform to the other's expectations; but instead, it would bring out the best of both partners and to unconditionally support each other to become the highest version of themselves and to live their supreme destiny.

Toshi thought about his kids. He realized that it didn't matter how much he thought he loved them or how he provided them with material comforts in life.

What mattered was how much love he gave them by giving them his time, his focused attention and his presence.

Toshi understood that when we are born, we are born with love and connected with God, with Source, with The Universe. Unfortunately, from that moment on, we are taught by the outside world we are not good enough as we are. This may come in the form of parents telling us we are not strong enough or that we need to improve grades in school. We are taught to make our physical appearances look better and to link our success and fulfillment with how much physical wealth we can gather in our lives.

We are taught not to focus on a power greater than ourselves but instead to focus on our physical world and on external validation, material wealth and success. We immediately learn about fear and are exposed to trauma, negative experiences and limiting beliefs about ourselves which blocks our 1st energy center. We are bombarded with distractions in our daily lives, and we are taught to compare ourselves with others who may have more than us, so we forget how to be present in the moment and how to be grateful for what we have, which blocks our 2nd energy center. We also make excuses for ourselves when we don't do our best by blaming others for our failures instead of taking responsibility for all our actions. This leads to a life of regret, which blocks our 3rd energy center. As we grow older, many of us get hurt in relationships or we compare our relationships to something unrealistic we see on TV, so we forget that we are worthy of love, respect and happiness, which blocks our 4th energy center. Since we are taught to value material wealth, we end up in jobs we are not passionate about, and we cannot find our true purpose in life, leading to a blockage in our 5th energy center. We forget how powerful we are and how we can manifest all our dreams, goals and desires into reality which leads to a blockage of our 6th energy center. Most importantly, we forget our connection with God, with Source, with the Universe, and we forget the importance of love which blocks our 7th energy center.

From the moment we are born, we experience events in our lives that prevent us from living to our highest potential. We are taught that the key to peace and fulfillment are things and material objects outside of us when the true key to lasting peace and fulfillment is Love and our connection with a power higher than ourselves, which we have always had within us from the moment we were born. Once we reconnect with God, with Source, with the Universe, we can finally understand this higher power has been guiding us towards our Supreme Destiny our whole lives.

Your Supreme Destiny

> *"There is a supreme moment of destiny calling on your life. Your job is to feel that, to hear that, to know that."*
> **–Oprah Winfrey**

Every person has a Supreme Destiny, which is a life where that person is living as their highest version of themselves and living to their fullest potential. The real question is not who you are right now but who you are meant to be. God, Source, The Universe is always trying to guide you toward your Supreme Destiny through your inner voice.

1. Listen to Your Inner Voice

> *"Behind every choice, the only real choice is between fear and love. Fear hurts and Love heals. Boil every choice down to what heals versus what hurts, answer fear with love and you will find the peace you seek."*
> **–A Course in Miracles made easy, Alan Cohen**

To connect with God, with Source, with the Universe, we must all listen to our inner voice. Every one of us has an inner voice that guides us to our Supreme Destiny. Some people call this inner voice the Holy Spirit, while others call this inner voice their intuition. Regardless of what you call it, messages from your inner voice are messages from a power higher and greater than ourselves, constantly guiding us to become the highest versions of ourselves physically, emotionally, mentally and spiritually. Your inner voice can also be messages you are receiving from loved ones who have passed away. Those loved ones are never gone because their love and energy are always present.

> *"Energy cannot be created or destroyed; it can only be changed from one form to another."*
> **–Albert Einstein**

Your loved ones are still with you, providing you guidance, love and protection in your inner voice or intuition. Toshi understood this voice has the answer to all your questions and is always open to guide you. You just have to listen.

How do you know whether the answers you receive are for your highest good? If the message is causing you to act out of love and causing you to feel love, then you know the message is from God, from Source, from The Universe. If the message is causing you to act out of fear and causing you to feel fear, then you know the message is from your Ego. You always choose the answer that leads to more love in the world. Therefore, it is so important to be present in the here and now, block out distractions and listen to that voice inside and allow God, allow Source, allow The Universe to guide you for your highest good.

> *"Protect your peace. Disconnect with the worldly distractions and Reconnect with your inner self."*

Your inner voice is always available to guide you. When you have a question, when you need something or when you need to know when is the right time to take action, all you need to do is ask God, ask Source, ask The Universe and be sure you are listening for the answer.

Sometimes we pray to God, or we ask the Universe for guidance, and we are disappointed because we feel it's a one-way dialogue. God, The Universe, Source is always communicating with us not only through our inner voice but also through synchronicities that appear in our lives. God is always giving us signs to motivate us, encourage us and tell us when we are on the right or wrong path. The signs and motivation can come in different forms and be something as small as seeing a butterfly at a time we are feeling discouraged or seeing repeating numbers or signs. There are never any coincidences, and each synchronistic event has a deeper meaning and lesson we must figure out.

Sometimes when you are not listening to your intuition, or you are letting your ego guide you instead, you get off track and may end up in an unfulfilling relationship or career. However, there are no failures in life.

Failure is God, is Source, is the Universe's way to tell you that you are off path and a reminder for you to act and proceed in a different direction so you can get back on track to reach your Supreme Destiny. As long as you always choose love and listen to your intuition and know that it comes from a source greater than yourself, there is never a wrong path because each path leads to your Supreme Destiny.

2. Trust That God Has a Purpose

> *"Life doesn't happen to you. It happens for you. Sometimes failing to reach your goal gives you your destiny."*
> **–Tony Robbins**

Toshi understood that God, Source, the Universe has a purpose for everything that has happened in our lives and for everything that will happen. You had to go through all your obstacles in life to get to this moment in your life. God, Source, the Universe has plans for you that you cannot even comprehend right now. If you have not achieved your dreams and goals yet in life, stay positive and trust that something bigger is planned for you. You are exactly where you are meant to be, and you are destined for something better because abundance in all aspects of your life is your birthright, and you will become the highest version of yourself and reach your fullest potential.

With this new understanding, Toshi was conscious of all the love and energy surrounding him. The Village was still quiet as the sun rose. Toshi walked back up the path and noticed the cherry blossom trees surrounding the field were in full bloom. Toshi walked past the trees into the open field, and as he reached the location of his sister's death, he saw someone standing across from him he hadn't seen since he was 18 years old. Although the man was much older now, Toshi could never forget those icy cold eyes and blank stare. He felt a chill run down his spine as it began to rain.

CHAPTER 10

The Samurai and The Power Of 7

The only sound you can hear is the deep breathing of the Samurai who has fallen to his knees in the open field surrounded by white and pink cherry blossoms that have slowly fallen from the Sakura trees above. He has trouble opening his left eye, not knowing if the sting is from the rain or from the blood dripping into it from the new wound on his head. His left hand is putting pressure on his abdomen, knowing he may breathe his last breaths, and yet he remains calm and even more determined. His right hand is clutching a katana, a sacred sword with the words, "Power of 7" surrounded by 7 circles engraved on the base of the blue-tinged blade, given to him by his father.

The village nearby is still quiet. The battle has gone on for some time now, and at this moment, neither Toshi or the hooded Samurai move an inch. Toshi knows he is losing blood fast and knows he has to use the principles of the Power of 7 to unleash one last strike using the remaining energy he has left.

Toshi closes his eyes and breathes deeply. He lets go of all the memories he had of his mother telling him he was too weak, too fragile and too small. He lets go of all the fear he felt the day his sister was killed, and he lets go of the anger and hatred he had in his heart for the hooded Samurai. At the same time, he is grateful that those experiences have made him into who he is at this moment. Toshi thinks about his sister and knows that he is safe, not alone and loved. Toshi feels the energy center at the base of his spine glow.

Toshi remembered the promise he made to himself when he was with the Architect that the next time he was in his village, he would take time to be fully present to appreciate the moment. Toshi grounds himself by looking up at the beautiful white and pink cherry blossoms surrounding him, which helps him understand, appreciate and accept the impermanence of life and the inevitability of death. He focuses on the feeling of the soft grass on his hands as he kneels on the field. He listens to the rustling of the cherry blossoms in the wind and the rain hitting the ground. He focuses on the metallic taste of the blood in his mouth, and he smells the aromas of the village as the villagers wake up and begin their day. Toshi is completely present in the moment and full of gratitude. He feels the energy center below his navel glowing.

Toshi knows that no matter what the outcome of this battle is, he will have no regrets. He has been preparing for this moment all his life, and this time, there would be no hesitation or fear. Toshi feels the energy in his solar plexus glowing.

Toshi felt no pressure or stress because he knew that win or lose, he was worthy of happiness, love and respect. The energy center in Toshi's heart glows bright.

He no longer accepts the unrealistic expectation of being the Samurai in Japan who never lost a battle. Instead, he knows he did his best, and he did not give up. He knows what his purpose is and there is no place else he would rather be in that moment. The energy center in Toshi's throat glows.

As Toshi stands up, he visualizes in his mind being in the presence of his wife and kids again. He sees their smiles and embraces them tightly. He visualizes spending time with his mother and the other villagers. He visualizes seeing himself happy, fulfilled and at peace. Toshi feels the hot glow of the energy center on his forehead.

Toshi feels God's presence with him, and he is filled with love. He looks at the hooded Samurai and forgives him, causing his 7th and final energy center in his crown to glow.

With the remaining energy that Toshi has left, he picks up his bamboo hat and places it on his head with his hair underneath flowing in the wind, free from the band that held up his top knot and his body free from any physical, mental, emotional or spiritual restrictions. He stands up tall and takes a reverse grip on his katana as the 7 energy centers continue to glow, vibrate and slowly form a circle surrounding him. At that moment, Toshi realizes that the Power of 7 was not just the release of the 7 energy centers within himself but also the energy and light he allowed himself to receive from all the loved ones in his life that gave him love and strength.

Toshi raises his Katana and charges at the hooded Samurai. When he is within striking distance, Toshi jumps and raises his sword over his head and makes a downward slash on the hooded Samurai at the exact moment the hooded Samurai delivers his final attack on Toshi. They both land on their feet facing the opposite direction. As Toshi stands there looking at the horizon, he feels blood dripping down the side of his body.

For the first time in his life, Toshi feels complete and at peace. Tears run down his face as he thinks of his wife and kids. He knows they will be proud of him. More importantly, he is proud of himself. He feels fulfilled. He did his best. He has no regrets.

EPILOGUE

The hooded Samurai was never seen again, and nobody knows what happened to the great Hitoshi Tabata after that day. Most people believed he and the hooded Samurai were both killed in battle. There were some who believe that Toshi survived and that he brought his wife and 5 children to meet his mother as he promised. They believe Toshi lived out the rest of his days following in the footsteps of his father, giving up fighting and living a purposeful and passionate life with his wife and children, telling them bedtime stories about Master Samurai and energy centers.

There was a small group, however, who believed that Toshi showed compassion in the last moment of the battle and spared the hooded Samurai's life. They believed that Toshi's act of forgiveness and kindness was something the hooded Samurai never experienced before, which caused him to change his ways and embark on his own journey to reach fulfillment.

Others suggest that the outcome of the battle was not relevant. They believed that what was important was that in those final moments, Toshi did the following:

1. Release the blockages in the base of his spine by Letting go of everything in his life that no longer served him,
2. Release the blockages below his navel by being completely present and grateful in the moment,
3. Release the blockages in his solar plexus by doing his best and having no regrets,
4. Release the blockages in his heart by knowing he was complete and worthy of love, happiness and respect,
5. Release the blockages in his throat by finding his purpose and following his passions,
6. Release the blockages of the area on his forehead between his eyes by knowing the power of his mind and the secret to manifesting his desires, dreams and goals into reality, and
7. Release the blockages in his crown by being fully connected with God and understanding that what is truly important in life is love.

In his final moments, Toshi had mastered the principles of the Power of 7 and had become the highest version of himself physically, mentally, emotionally and spiritually, successfully reaching his fullest potential and living his Supreme Destiny. He was happy, he was fulfilled, he was at peace, he was connected to God, and he was filled with LOVE.

ABOUT THE AUTHOR

Robert G. Chu is a Judge for the Los Angeles County Superior Court in California. He was a criminal trial lawyer for the Los Angeles County Public Defender's Office for 12 years before he was appointed to the bench by Governor Jerry Brown in 2018. He received his B.A. from the University of California Los Angeles and received his Juris Doctor from Southwestern University School of Law. He is married with 5 children and has a passion for helping others see their inner power and strength. He teaches Brazilian Jiu-jitsu to kids in the community to empower them to have self-confidence.

Made in United States
North Haven, CT
30 June 2025